ROYAL BOROUGH OF GREENWICH

Follow us on twitter 🐦 @greenwichlibs

RE

Please return by the last date shown

Thank you! To renew, please contact any
Royal Greenwich library or renew online at
www.better.org.uk/greenwichlibraries

PICK OF THE BEST

CHESS PROBLEMS

Compiled by

B. P. BARNES

PAPERFRONTS
ELLIOT RIGHT WAY BOOKS
KINGSWOOD, SURREY, U.K.

Made and Printed by Love and Malcomson, Redhill, Surrey, U.K.

Contents

Introduction

The chess problems in this book obey explicitly the rules of chess. If you know the moves of the pieces, solving the problems will be well within your capabilities. In any case, difficulty of solution is not the main criterion. Rather, the pleasure of problem chess lies in an appreciation of how White wins. There are no dull draws here – only exciting mate finishes!

'White to play and mate in two moves' is the stipulation for all of the problems. This means that White plays first, and, having made the one and only correct first move (the *key*), White is able to mate Black on his second move whatever defensive move Black makes. For example, in the following diagram –

B. P. Barnes
First Publication

White to play and mate in two moves

– the only move which solves the problem is the sweeping key 1 Rh3! to threaten 2 Rh8 mate. Black can muster four defences, but against each the white Rook (c7) and the white Bishop (f4) line-up (a B+R *battery*) can open four times on the file to mate, and therein lies the unity of this small problem. The full written solution is –

> Key 1 Rh3! (threat 2 Rh8 mate)
> 1 ... Pe3+ 2 Rxc2 mate
> 1 ... Bb3 or a4 2 Rxc1 mate
> 1 ... Bb2 2 Rc3 mate
> 1 ... Ba3 2 Rc5 mate

A move which almost solves the problem (a *try*) is 1 aRc3? This threatens 2 Rc8 double-check mate, but 1 ... Pe3+! saves Black as the Rook (c7) cannot clear the obstruction at c3 and parry the check with a capture of the black Bishop (c2). Another try which fails more obviously is 1 Rd3? (threatening 2 Rd8 mate), but 1 ... Pxd3! Such *tries* are an important element of problem chess since they help to disguise the true solution, and add to the solver's enjoyment.

In case you are not familiar with the *algebraic notation* of recording piece names, squares and moves on the chess board, this is explained in a separate section.

Now some words about the type of problems in this collection. They all have not more than 12 pieces and not less than 8, and are a traditionally popular type known as *Merediths*. They take their name from William Meredith, an American composer, who built a lasting reputation for making such relatively lightweight problems towards the end of the last century. There is no special magic about the numerical limitations of 12 and 8, but 'not more than 12 pieces' imposes on problem composers an extra special discipline to show their ideas within that maximum, and not to settle easily for, say, 13 pieces. Economy of expression is as important in problem chess as it is in other art forms.

The 200 selected problems are all by British composers, and represent an *anthology of the best British Merediths*. You will be astonished at the depth and variety of the ideas shown, many of which you have never seen and never will see in over-the-board play.

To chess players, many of the positions will seem implausible, but it is a requirement of problemists that their compositions be legal positions. However improbable the grouping of the pieces or the material odds, each problem position can be reached by imaginary play from the initial game array. Strong links are preserved with the game.

In addition to the 'White to play and mate in two moves' stipulation beneath each diagram, there is a caption. Should you decide to solve any of the problems which are arranged in meaningful pairs, the light-hearted captions (forgive some bad puns) might or might not provide clues! Whatever your approach, there are full solutions and explanatory notes.

You will be in good company with chess problems. V. Lenin relaxed with problem chess; the late Dr. Bronowski's remarkable intellect extended to an appreciation of problem composition; and author V. Nabokov is not sufficiently distracted by his naughty Lolita to forget the charms of the chess board.

I wish you many happy hours.

Explanation of Algebraic Notation

1 P–K4 P–K4 2 N–KB3 N–QB3 3 B–B4 B–B4 is the *descriptive notation* familiar to players, but the six moves' conversion to 1 Pe4 Pe5 2 Sf3 Sc6 3Bc4 Bc5 is the *algebraic notation* of chess problemists universally. Unlike descriptive, algebraic notation sees all squares and moves from White's point of view. As will be seen from the accompanying diagram, the ranks (horizontal rows of squares) are numbered 1 to 8, starting with the rank where White's pieces begin the game. The files (vertical rows of squares) are lettered a to h, from left to right. The pieces are given letters: K=King, Q=Queen, R=Rook, B=Bishop, S=Knight and P=Pawn. The 'S' used for *Knight is* derived from the German 'Springer'.

When a capture is made, algebraic notation shows on which square the capture takes place, rather than what piece is taken. Thus if Black has Rooks on a1 and a8 which can capture a white Bishop on a5, the capture by the BRa8 is written 8Rxa5. The symbol + is used for check. Castling is written 0–0 (King's Rook) or 0–0–0 (Queen's Rook).

Hints for Solving Two-Move Problems

By convention, chess problem diagrams are printed so that White is to play up the board. White plays first, and the move order for 'mate in two' problems is 1 White Black 2 White mates. The correct and first White move is the *key*; Black moves are *defences*; and the White second moves are mates. The black defences and the appropriate white mates are *variations* in the whole of the play which is the *solution*. If the problem cannot be solved in the stipulated two moves, it is said to have *No Solution*. If, by an oversight of the composer, more than one first move solves the problem, there is a *cook*, and the problem is spoilt. *Set play* referred to in the solutions is no more than the mating possibilities in the diagrammed position.

Imagine that each problem is the final stage of a game, and that you have the definite assurance that there is a mate in two moves. You would be ashamed of yourself if you missed such a quick finish, so marshal your thoughts and solve the problem no matter what defences Black makes to a key-move which is there. Of course, some keys and the means of mating Black will not be obvious, but tell yourself that check-mate is only two moves away — and find it!

In your search for the key, study the position of the Black King. Can the Black King move as in *2* to d7, a *flight-square*, without White being able to make a mating reply? So the key 1 Pe4! threatens 2 Rd5, a mating move which takes into account d7, and provides for 1 ... Kd7 by 2 Rd5 mate. However, a key will sometimes grant more flight-squares as in *87* to gain advantage. Can Black destroy White's guards on the squares immediately surrounding the Black King? 1 ... Sf4 to provide the Black King with flight-squares at f3 and f2 in *142* is a clue to the key 1 Qb4! which provides for 1 ... Sf4 by 2 Bd4 mate. Is there need for White to release the Black King from a stalemate position as in *55*? As there is supposed to be nothing superfluous on the board, is there any White piece so placed that it must move or be brought into play by the move of another White piece if it is to play its part in the check-mate of the Black King? Does the WBg2 or the WSg4 move in *174* to bring the distant WRg1 into play, as well as provide for the flights by the Black King to g6 and g8? Must White provide for a subtle but strong move by Black such as 1 ... Qg7+ which checks White disastrously if the WRe5 makes any move but 1 Re3! in *86*?

In chess problems, as in the game, White can impose a check-mate on Black either by finding a move to threaten mate or, more subtly, by putting Black in *Zugzwang* i.e. threatening no immediate mate, but putting Black in such a position that Black must move and incur a fatal weakness. Therefore, you need to find key-moves which either threaten immediate mate or simply wait. The threat problems are usually easier to recognise. For example, in *82* there are so many inconsequential moves (1 ... Qa1/a2/b1/c1 etc) which create no weakness in Black's position that a threat from White is clearly necessary to harry Black.

As in most other fields of endeavour, practical experience counts. Set up a chess problem on a board, and slave away until you solve it. In this way, the composer's art will be revealed, and your enjoyment of chess problems will increase beyond all expectations. With that in mind, you may expect the unexpected in this art form where paradox is commonplace!

200 Selected
Meredith Problems

1 LADIES FIRST

Mrs. W. J. Baird
'Illust. Sporting & Dramatic
News' c. 1902

*White to play and mate in
two moves*

2 WOMANLY WILES

Mrs. T. B. Rowland
'Wesley College Quarterly'
1889

*White to play and mate in
two moves*

3 WALL UP THE ROOK!

E. J. Winter-Wood
'v. Land & Water'
c. 1886

*White to play and mate in
two moves*

4 BURY THE BISHOP!

G. Heathcote
'Tidskrift'
1910

*White to play and mate in
two moves*

5 25% CLAIMED 'NO SOLUTION'

P. H. Williams
'Chess Amateur'
1910

*White to play and mate in
two moves*

6 CAN/CANNOT CASTLE

N. A. Macleod
'The Problemist'
1973

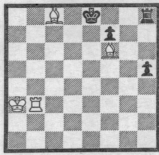

*White to play and mate in
two moves*
Position (*a*) As Diagram
Position (*b*) Remove BPh5

7 BEGINNER'S LUCK

R. Gray
'Glasgow Herald'
1932

*White to play and mate in
two moves*

8 WHITE MAKES BLACK CROSS

B. G. Laws
HM 'Jamaica Family
Journal' 1881

*White to play and mate in
two moves*

9 TOO MUCH HORSE-PLAY?

T. Salthouse
'London Globe'
1911

*White to play and mate in
two moves*

10 BLACK'S TURN TO PROMOTE

C. G. Watney
'Observer'
1920

*White to play and mate in
two moves*

11 CHECK AND COUNTER-CHECK

N. Easter
'The Problemist'
1929

*White to play and mate in
two moves*

12 A LOVELY PAIR!

G. F. Anderson
'Il Secolo'
1919

*White to play and mate in
two moves*

13 MUTUAL INTERFERENCE

A. W. Daniel
'British Chess Magazine'
1952

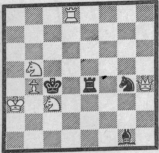

White to play and mate in two moves

14 WHITE TRIPS UP

L. S. Penrose
'British Chess Magazine'
1947

White to play and mate in two moves

15 ONE OVER THE EIGHT!

C. Mansfield
'Morning Post'
1933

White to play and mate in two moves

16 THOROUGHLY MODERN MÊLÉE

N. A. Macleod
HM 'American Chess Bulletin' 1954

White to play and mate in two moves

17 THE QUEEN GOES FREE

A. R. Gooderson
'The Field'
1963

White to play and mate in two moves

18 MITIGATING CIRCUMSTANCES

E. Boswell
2nd Comm.
'The Problemist' 1926

White to play and mate in two moves

19 DIVERSIONARY TACTICS

A. J. Fenner
'Chess'
1936

White to play and mate in two moves

20 THE GREAT LEAP BACKWARD

J. C. Evans
'British Chess Magazine'
1914

White to play and mate in two moves

21 BOTH SOLUTIONS ARE RIGHT!

W. Langstaff
'Chess Amateur'
1922

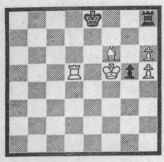

White to play and mate in two moves

22 WHY CAN'T BLACK CASTLE?

R. I. Gunn
'Chess'
1941

White to play and mate in two moves

23 FORCE THE PACE

P. Barron
'Chess'
1951

White to play and mate in two moves

24 ATTACK IS BEST FORM OF DEFENCE

T. & J. Warton
'Morning Post'
1917

White to play and mate in two moves

25 KINGPIN
B. J. de C. Andrade
2nd Comm.
'The Problemist' 1942

*White to play and mate in
two moves*

**26 THE POWER BE-
HIND THE THRONE**
M. Lipton
(version by G. Jönsson)
1st HM Ring Ty.
'Evening News' 1958

*White to play and mate in
two moves*

27 KING KEY
G. F. Anderson
1st Pr. e.a. 'South African
CP Society Meredith Ty'
1946/7

*White to play and mate in
two moves*

28 FLEDG-LING!
J. F. Ling
'Chess'
1942

*White to play and mate in
two moves*

29 TOP RANK ENTERTAINMENT!

H. M. Cuttle
'Chess Amateur'
1926

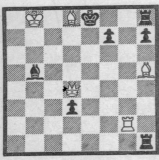

White to play and mate in two moves

30 MATED IN THE BACK ROW

D. W. A. Brotherton
2nd Pr. '2nd McWilliam Ty,
The Problemist' 1955

White to play and mate in two moves

31 OUT OF CONTROL

B. J. de C. Andrade
'British Chess Magazine'
1958

White to play and mate in two moves

32 ON HIS MAJESTY'S SERVICE

C. Mansfield
2nd Pr. 'British Chess
Federation Ty' 1927

White to play and mate in two moves

33 TAKES TWO TO TANGLE

G. C. Alvey
'Surrey Weekly Press'
1919

White to play and mate in two moves

34 GRIMSHAW

D. A. Smedley
3rd Pr. 'The Problemist'
1957

White to play and mate in two moves

35 TWEEDLEDUM AND TWEEDLEDEE

E. Stevenson
'British Chess Magazine'
1941

White to play and mate in two moves

36 FOUR HANDS ROUND

R. A. Batchelor
1st Pr. 'Our Own Composers, The Problemist' 1964

White to play and mate in two moves

37 CORRECTIVE MEASURES

N. A. Macleod
'Chess World'
1947

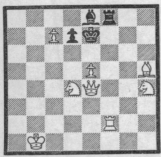

White to play and mate in two moves

38 NEW MATES FOR OLD?

J. M. Rice
'Correspondence Chess'
1958

White to play and mate in two moves

39 A LOW-DOWN DIVE

J. Keeble
(version by F. B. Feast)
'Leeds Mercury'
1888

White to play and mate in two moves

40 . . . . . DIVIDED WE FALL

B. P. Barnes
'British Chess Magazine'
1970

White to play and mate in two moves
Two solutions

41 *WHAT GOES UP . . .*
J. F. Ling
'The Problemist'
1968

*White to play and mate in
two moves*

42 *. . . MUST COME DOWN!*
A. G. Stubbs
1st Pr. 'Good Companions'
1923

*White to play and mate in
two moves*

43 *CAT AND MOUSE SITUATION*
W. Gleave
'English Mechanic'
1891

*White to play and mate in
two moves*

44 *TOP CAT AND MOUSE SITUATION!*
M. Lipton
5th HM 'Probleemblad'
1957

*White to play and mate in
two moves*

45 *UP THE JUNCTION!*
F. Healey
v. 'FH Collection of Chess
Problems'
1866

*White to play and mate in
two moves*

46 *WHITE MAKES
CUTTING POINTS!*
M. Lipton
2nd Pr. Ring Ty.
'Sunday Citizen' 1966

*White to play and mate in
two moves*

47 *LONG-RANGE
INTERFERENCE*
J. Montgomerie
'British Chess Magazine'
1955

*White to play and mate in
two moves*

48 *FORECLOSURES*
C. G. Rains
'Observer'
1939

*White to play and mate in
two moves*

49 PERCY BLAKE? SEXTON BLAKE!

P. F. Blake
'The Field' No. 2838
Date?

*White to play and mate in
two moves*

50 IN THE OLD-FASHIONED WAY

P. F. Blake
Where?
prior to 1897

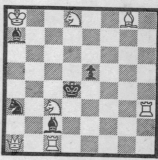

*White to play and mate in
two moves*

51 A 17 YEAR OLD DOYEN!

G. W. Chandler
'Hobbies'
1907

*White to play and mate in
two moves*

52 THE DISAPPEARING TRICK

R. A. Batchelor
'The Problemist'
1964

*White to play and mate in
two moves*

53 SIGNS OF INTELLIGENCE
F. H. Guest
'Chess Bouquet' 1897

White to play and mate in two moves

54 INTUITIVE BEGINNINGS
T. Taverner
'Chess Bouquet' 1897

White to play and mate in two moves

55 WHAT A RELIEF!
P. Grimshaw
'Chess Amateur' 1920

White to play and mate in two moves

56 THE LONE RANGER
C. Mansfield
'The Problemist' 1959

White to play and mate in two moves

(e) WKc8 to e2	Position (a) As diagram
(f) WKe2 to f2	(b) WKb4 to b5
(g) WKf2 to h4	(c) WKb5 to b7
(h) WKh4 to h7	(d) WKb7 to c8

←

57 CLASSIC FOCAL PLAY

C. Mansfield
'Morning Post'
1923

White to play and mate in two moves

58 BREAK THE BISHOP'S GRIP

N. A. Macleod
5th HM Ring Ty.
'Correspondence Chess'
1962

White to play and mate in two moves

59 VICE VERSA

B. P. Barnes
'Sunday Times'
1964

White to play and mate in two moves

60 ABBA

J. M. Rice
'Correspondence Chess'
1961

White to play and mate in two moves

61 A PAWN IN THE GAME

T. M. Stott
'British Chess Magazine'
1944

White to play and mate in two moves

62 PICKANINNY

C. Mansfield
3rd Pr. Segal Memorial Ty.
'Themes 64'
1962

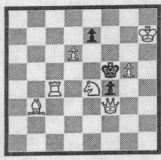

White to play and mate in two moves

63 TOP OF THE FORM

A. C. Challenger
'Schoolmaster'
1895

White to play and mate in two moves

64 BATTLE ROYAL

D. M. Davey
'The Tablet'
1952

White to play and mate in two moves

65 DON'T ALL RUSH

R. L. Wynne
'The Problemist'
1940

White to play and mate in two moves

66 LEGAL SEPARATION

C. Mansfield
Comm. 'British Chess
Magazine' 1966

White to play and mate in two moves

67 CURIOUSER AND CURIOUSER

W. Langstaff
2nd Pr. 'Good Companions'
1924

White to play and mate in two moves

68 GOETHART UNPINS

B. P. Barnes
1st. Comm.
'Dt. Schachblatter'
1963

White to play and mate in two moves

69 PASSED OVER PAWN

C. Mansfield
'Observer'
1946

White to play and mate in two moves

70 SAME BUT DIFFERENT!

T. R. Dawson
'British Chess Magazine'
1947

White to play and mate in two moves

71 TWO UNPINS OF A BISHOP

R. G. Thomson
HM 'Grantham Journal'
1926

White to play and mate in two moves

72 GRANDMASTER CLASS

C. Mansfield
1st. Pr. 'Austral
Meredith Ty' 1928

White to play and mate in two moves

73 WHICH KNIGHT MOVES AND WHERE?

B. P. BARNES
Comm. 'British Chess
Magazine' 1961

*White to play and mate in
two moves*

74 WHICH ROOK MOVES AND WHERE?

B. P. Barnes
'Skakbladet'
1961

*White to play and mate in
two moves*

75 LUCKY SEVEN!

J. M. Rice
2nd HM
'British Chess Magazine'
1965

*White to play and mate in
two moves*

76 COMBINATIVE SEPARATION

J. M. Rice
'Die Schwalbe'
1965

*White to play and mate in
two moves*

B

77 CHANGED SELF-PINS

C. Mansfield
'Chess Life'
1956

White to play and mate in two moves

78 A CHESS PROBLEM TABOO

M. Lipton
'Schakend Nederland'
1967

White to play and mate in two moves

79 IS BLACK IN A TIGHT CORNER?

C. Mansfield
'Observer'
1919

White to play and mate in two moves

80 ONCE A KNIGHT!

Rev. E. C. Mortimer
'The Problemist'
1942

White to play and mate in two moves

81 *RUNNING THE GAUNTLET*

G. Hume
'Letts Household
Magazine' 1884

*White to play and mate in
two moves*

82 *PAWN'S GAMBIT*

D. Pirnie
'British Chess Magazine'
1917

*White to play and mate in
two moves*

83 *AN OPEN AND SHUT
CASE*

C. E. Kemp
'British Chess Magazine'
1933

*White to play and mate in
two moves*

84 *CHESS CHAMPION'S
PROBLEM*

D. B. Pritchard
'British Chess Magazine'
1943

*White to play and mate in
two moves*

85 *A QUEEN INTERPOSES*

F. B. Feast
'Hampstead Express'
1914

White to play and mate in two moves

86 *INTELLIGENT ANTICIPATION*

D. Mackay
'Observer'
1920

White to play and mate in two moves

87 *AN OLD-TIME SPECIAL*

A. C. Challenger
'Knowledge'
1898

White to play and mate in two moves

88 *AT A STROKE!*

J. Bunting
'To Alain White'
1945

White to play and mate in two moves

89 DON'T CHEER TOO SOON

F. W. Andrew
'British Chess Magazine'
1904

White to play and mate in two moves

90 LEVMANN DEFENCES

T. R. Dawson
'British Chess Magazine'
1947

White to play and mate in two moves

91 POTENT PAWNS

B. Harley
'Morning Post'
1933

White to play and mate in two moves

92 IDEAS ABOVE HIS STATION!

B. W. Dennis
'The Problemist'
1969

White to play and mate in two moves

93 SOLVERS OUT-GUNNED?

R. I. Gunn
'Chess'
1944

*White to play and mate in
two moves*

94 CASTLES IN THE AIR!

C. S. Kipping
'Falkirk Herald'
1923

*White to play and mate in
two moves*

95 WHY NOT P=Q CHECK?

B. J. de C. Andrade
'The Problemist'
1941

*White to play and mate in
two moves*

96 TOO CLEVER BY HALF?

F. B. Allen
'British Chess Magazine'
1938

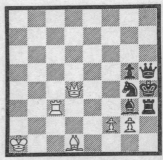

*White to play and mate in
two moves*

97 DRAW OFF THE CAVALRY

S. Sedgwick
'British Chess Magazine'
1958

White to play and mate in two moves

98 EASTER EGGS YOU ON!

N. Easter
1st HM 'Bristol Times &
Mirror' 1928

White to play and mate in two moves

99 ALBINO

E. Woodard
'P.G.T.'
1915

White to play and mate in two moves

100 ALBINO TWINS

Sir Jeremy Morse
'Correspondence Chess'
1962

White to play and mate in two moves

101 SHE STOOPS TO CONQUER
P. H. Williams
'Chess Amateur'
1917

102 SMALL CHANGE
P. H. Williams
'Chess Amateur'
1915

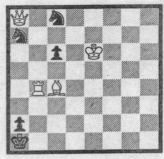

White to play and mate in
two moves

White to play and mate in
two moves

103 INITIALLY 'JB'
JB of Bridport
'Illustrated London News'
1863

104 POLISHED OFF
G. Heathcote
1st Pr. 'English Mechanic'
1891

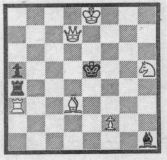

White to play and mate in
two moves

White to play and mate in
two moves

105 *PAST MASTER*
G. J. Slater
HM 'Western Daily Mercury'
1907

*White to play and mate in
two moves*

106 *UP FOR GRABS*
J. Stewart
'Young Scotland'
1940

*White to play and mate in
two moves*

107 *HINGES ON
SQUARE B1*
H. W. Grant
1st Pr. 'Australasian
Column' 1924

*White to play and mate in
two moves*

108 *THE RIGHT
APPROACH!*
M. Lipton
'Schakend Nederland'
1968

*White to play and mate in
two moves*

109 PRECISION PLAY
H. Bristow
'Chess Miniatures'
Date?

*White to play and mate in
two moves*

110 THE ROOKERY
J. L. Rendall
'The Field'
1955

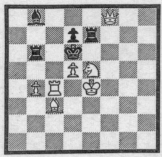

*White to play and mate in
two moves*

111 THE THIRD-
DIMENSION
A. C. Reeves
3rd HM 'Cs. Sach'
1963

*White to play and mate in
two moves*

112 ZAGORUJKO
J. E. Driver
First Publication

*White to play and mate in
two moves*

113 OUT OF THE BLUE
A. G. Stubbs
2nd Pr. 'Good Companions
7th Meredith Ty'
1918

*White to play and mate in
two moves*

114 VARIATIONS ON A THEME
C. Mansfield
Comm. 'Sachovy Kutik
Meredith Ty'
1964

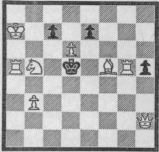

*White to play and mate in
two moves*

115 THE LITTLE NUISANCE
E. Westbury
2nd HM 'Good Companions
5th Meredith Ty' 1917

*White to play and mate in
two moves*

116 NO FRILLS
A. R. Gooderson
'Time & Tide'
1954

*White to play and mate in
two moves*

117 *NOW YOU SEE IT, NOW YOU DON'T*

N. A. Macleod
'Chess World'
1950

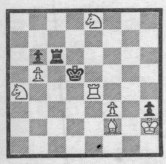

White to play and mate in two moves

118 *RUKHLIS*

M. Lipton
'Israel Ring Ty'
1963

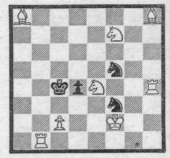

White to play and mate in two moves

119 *A DEVILISH TRY*

S. W. Eckett
'Bath & Wilts.
Chronicle & Herald'
1947

White to play and mate in two moves

120 *BLACK CORRECTION*

D. Shire
'British Chess Magazine'
1973

White to play and mate in two moves

121 ...WHERE ANGELS FEAR TO TREAD

A. Guest
'Chess Bouquet'
1897

White to play and mate in two moves

122 A MEASURED TREAD

T. R. Dawson
'British Chess Magazine'
1942

White to play and mate in two moves

123 WHAT WE WANT

G. C. Watney & B. Harley
'Chess Pie'
1922

White to play and mate in two moves

124 INTO THE THICK OF IT

B. P. Barnes
2nd Pr. Ring Ty.
'Evening News'
Brian Harley Award 1959

White to play and mate in two moves

125 ROTARY INTERNATIONAL

C. Mansfield
1st Pr. Ring Ty
'Correspondence Chess' 1958

White to play and mate in two moves

126 A HORSE OF A DIFFERENT COLOUR!

A. C. Reeves
3rd HM Ring Ty
'The Tablet' 1962

White to play and mate in two moves

127 FLY AWAY PETER . . .

A. C. Reeves
'Problem'
1965

White to play and mate in two moves

128 . . . COME BACK PAUL!

C. P. Sydenham
'British Chess Magazine'
1975

White to play and mate in two moves

129 COUNT DOWN
J. M. Rice
'British Chess Magazine'
1965

*White to play and mate in
two moves*

130 HALF A DOZEN OF ONE ...
M. Lipton
'Sinfonie Scacchistiche'
1966

*White to play and mate in
two moves*

131 AMBUSH!
F. B. Feast
Source?

*White to play and mate in
two moves*

132 THE OBLIQUE APPROACH
J. L. Peake
'Observer'
1959

*White to play and mate in
two moves*

133 WYNNE FOR WHITE!

F. W. Wynne
1st Pr. 'Birmingham News'
1903

White to play and mate in two moves

134 BANK ON SIR JEREMY!

Sir Jeremy Morse
'British Chess Magazine'
1962

White to play and mate in two moves

135 BRIDGE THAT GAP!

P. F. Blake
2nd. Pr. 'Kentish Mercury'
1898

White to play and mate in two moves

136 PENNY FOR HIS THOUGHTS!

A. C. Challenger
'Penny Illustrated Paper'
1895

White to play and mate in two moves

137 NEAR SYMMETRY
C. Mansfield
1st HM 'British Chess
Magazine' 1933

*White to play and mate in
two moves*

138 OUT OF FOCUS
N. A. Macleod
'Parallele 50'
1951

*White to play and mate in
two moves*

139 MASKED HALF-
BATTERY
C. Mansfield
'Die Schwalbe'
1964

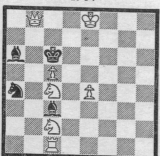

*White to play and mate in
two moves*

140 GRAND
CLEARANCE
A. C. Reeves
'The Problemist'
1966

*White to play and mate in
two moves*
Position (a) As diagram
Position (b) BPg7 to c7

141 OFF PAT
W. A. Clark
(version by W. Marks)
3rd Pr. 'Schoolmaster'
1891

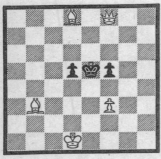

White to play and mate in two moves

142 GIVES THE GAME AWAY?
C. D. Locock
'Knowledge'
1896

White to play and mate in two moves

143 MAKE WAY FOR HER MAJESTY!
F. B. Feast
v. 1st Pr. 'Good Companions' 1924

White to play and mate in two moves

144 YOU WILL BE EXTERMINATED!
N. A. Macleod
'Sunday Times'
1958

White to play and mate in two moves

145 MASTER MASTER ANDERSON!
G. F. Anderson
'Natal Mercury'
1914

White to play and mate in two moves

146 WHITE GIVES UP!
B. G. Laws
(version by F. B. Feast)
1st Pr. 'Jamaica Gleaner'
1892

White to play and mate in two moves

147 NICE MATIN–G!
E. W. Beal
'Nice Matin'
1972

White to play and mate in two moves

148 BITING THE HAND THAT FEEDS
Dom. J. Coombe-Tennant
'Diagrammes'
1975

White to play and mate in two moves

149 RECORD BREAKER?

M. Lipton
1st HM 'Observer' 1966

*White to play and mate in
two moves*

150 WITHDRAWAL METHOD!

B. P. Barnes
'Correspondence Chess' 1957

*White to play and mate in
two moves*

151 THROUGH THE LOOKING-GLASS

C. S. Kipping
'Chess Amateur' 1923

*White to play and mate in
two moves*
Position (*a*) As diagram
Position (*b*) Reflect from
right to left

152 WHITE'S MOVE TO TURN!

B. P. Barnes
'The Tablet' 1961

*White to play and mate in
two moves*
Position (*a*) As diagram
Position (*b*) Quarter turn
anti-clockwise

153 RED INDIAN . . .
J. Laybourn
'Nationaltidende'
1891

*White to play and mate in
two moves*

154 . . . SLAUGHTERS WHITES!
A. C. Challenger
'The Morning'
1897

*White to play and mate in
two moves*

155 DOUBLE DOUBLE-CHECK BUT MATE!
E. S. Campling
v. 'British Chess Magazine'
1901

*White to play and mate in
two moves*

156 WHITE DOUBLE DOUBLE-CHECKS
C. Mansfield
1st Pr. 'Falkirk Herald
Meredith Ty' 1927

*White to play and mate in
two moves*

157 OF PRIME SECOND-ARY IMPORTANCE!

C. Mansfield
3rd Pr. 'Chess World
Meredith Ty' 1946

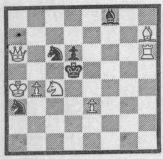

*White to play and mate in
two moves*

158 ONE DEGREE OVER

J. M. Rice & M. Lipton
'Problem'
1957

*White to play and mate in
two moves*

159 USING THE WHITE KING

C. Vaughan
1st HM 'American Chess
Bulletin Meredith Ty' 1950

*White to play and mate in
two moves*

160 EXPERTS BEWARE!

H. D'O. Bernard
'Cape Times'
1938

*White to play and mate in
two moves*

161 LINE CLOSURES
N. Easter
'British Chess Magazine'
1932

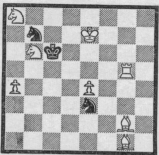

White to play and mate in two moves

162 DETERMINED ON PROMOTION!
P. C. Thomson
'Echíquier de Paris' 1954

White to play and mate in two moves

163 CHOICE OF PIN/UNPIN
M. Lipton
'Il Due Mosse' 1959

White to play and mate in two moves

164 DO MEANS JUSTIFY END?
C, Vaughan
'The Problemist' 1966

White to play and mate in two moves
Position (*a*) As diagram
Position (*b*) Replace WSg4
with WB, and move WPa2 to b2

165 KEYED UP

J. W. Abbott
'Illustrated London News'
1886

*White to play and mate in
two moves*

166 CUT IT OUT!

A. W. Busby
1st Pr. 'Sunday Chronicle'
1940

*White to play and mate in
two moves*

167 INVOLUNTARY
REACTION

C. Mansfield
'British Chess Magazine'
1936

*White to play and mate in
two moves*

168 SMEDLEY MEDLEY

D. A. Smedley
'The Problemist'
1952

*White to play and mate in
two moves*

169 WING FORWARD!
C. Mansfield
'Observer'
1941

White to play and mate in
two moves

170 PASSIVE RESISTANCE
R. A. Tappenden
'Sunday Times'
1919

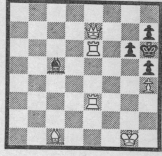

White to play and mate in
two moves

171 UPPER AND A DOWNER!
G. R. Downer
'The Problemist'
1941

White to play and mate in
two moves

172 ETERNAL TRIANGLE
W. F. Wills
'Norwich Mercury Ty'
1902/3

White to play and mate in
two moves

173 BLACK SEES STARS!

J. M. Rice
2nd Pr. 'Dutch Problem
Society Jubilee Ty' 1961

*White to play and mate in
two moves*

174 PROCESS OF LOGIC?

B. P. Barnes
'L'Italia Scacchistica'
1961

*White to play and mate in
two moves*

175 NICE ONE, CYRIL!

C. S. Kipling
'The Problemist'
1951

*White to play and mate in
two moves*

176 DUEL TO THE DEATH

G. C. Quack
'The Problemist'
1967

*White to play and mate in
two moves*

177 HALF-PIN DEMONSTRATION

D. A. Smedley
'The Problemist'
1958

White to play and mate in two moves

178 GREAT RE-DISCOVERY

C. Mansfield
1st HM 'Good Companions
8th Meredith Ty'1918

White to play and mate in two moves

179 UNIQUE COMBINATION?

B. P. Barnes
Comm. 'The Problemist'
1974

White to play and mate in two moves

180 OUT OF THE RUNNING?

B. P. Barnes
'The Problemist'
1962

White to play and mate in two moves

181 THE FRENCH CONNECTION

N. A. Macleod
Comm. 'Probleme Theme Ty'
1966

White to play and mate in two moves

182 TAKEN TO TASK

Sir Jeremy Morse
'The Problemist'
1964

White to play and mate in two moves

183 UNDERHAND TRICKS!

A. Townsend
'Gentleman's Journal'
c. 1870

White to play and mate in two moves
Position (*a*) As diagram
Position (*b*) Remove BPf7

184 STILL GOING STRONG

C. Mansfield
'40 Dubbele Task
Problemen' 1962

White to play and mate in two moves

185 MUCH ADO ABOUT NOTHING!

JB of Bridport
1850–1865
Source?

White to play and mate in two moves

186 ANCIENT BRITONS

F. Healey
'Dt. Schachzeitung'
1887

White to play and mate in two moves

187 NO WANDERING MINSTREL HE!

C. Mansfield
2nd Pr. 'Falkirk Herald
Meredith Ty' 1932

White to play and mate in two moves

188 OLD SCHOOL TIE

W. T. Hurley
'The Williamsonian'
1918

White to play and mate in two moves

189 MUTATION

P. S. Healey
(version by F. B. Feast)
'British Chess Magazine'
1918

*White to play and mate in
two moves*

190 IT MAKES A CHANGE!

H. D'O. Bernard
HM 'Chess Amateur'
1918

*White to play and mate in
two moves*

191 THE SIDEBOARD KEY!

H. D'O. Bernard
'Chess Amateur'
1919

*White to play and mate in
two moves*

192 FOUR-WAY-PLAY

B. N. Lewis
4th Comm.
'Stratford Express'
1949

*White to play and mate in
two moves*

193 TELL TALE ROOK
E. J. Eddy
'The Problemist'
1943

194 GIVE A LITTLE, TAKE A LITTLE
N. A. Macleod
'Observer'
1962

White to play and mate in two moves

White to play and mate in two moves

195 WAS HE FIRST?
A. M. Sparke
1st Pr.'Good Companions Meredith Ty' 1918

196 ASSOCIATION OF IDEAS
C. Mansfield
'The Problemist'
1956

White to play and mate in two moves

White to play and mate in two moves

197 DISTURBING THE PIECE!

C. P. Sydenham
'Probleemblad'
1976

White to play and mate in two moves

198 SAFETY PINS

C. P. Sydenham
1st Pr. 'Y. Cheylan
Theme Ty'
1976

White to play and mate in two moves

199 DEDICATED TO LONDON TRANSPORT

B. P. Barnes
'Busmen's Chess Review'
1962

White to play and mate in two moves

200 LATE DEVELOPMENT PAYS!

B. Harley
'Observer'
1926

White to play and mate in two moves

Solutions and Commentaries

1 LADIES FIRST

> Key 1 Qe2! Waiting
> 1 ... Kd5 2 Sb4 mate
> 1 ... Pb4 2 Sf4 mate
> 1 ... Pd5 2 Qc2 mate
> 1 ... S any 2 Qe4 mate

With more than 2,000 problems to her credit, Mrs. W. J. Baird (1859–1924) was the best known and certainly the most prolific of the world's relatively few *women composers*. She came from the distinguished chess-playing family, the Winter-Woods, and, in turn, her daughter, Lilian Baird, achieved fame as a problem composer at a very early age.

With no complex interaction of the pieces and no deep-laid plans, the problem is simple by today's standards.

2 WOMANLY WILES

> Key 1 Pe4! (threat 2 Rd5 mate)
> 1 ... Kd7 2 Rd5 mate
> 1 ... dPxe4 en passant 2 Qd1 mate
> 1 ... fPxe4 en passant 2 Qxd4 mate
> 1 ... Re5 2 Ra6 mate
> 1 ... Rxe4 2 Sxe4 mate
> 1 ... Re8+ 2 Pxe8=S mate

Again, chess was in the family with Mr. T. B. Rowland being a problemist as well as an author of several chess problem books, but Mrs. Rowland (née F. F. Beechey) seems to have had the edge on her husband! Her problem became widely known for its striking *en passant* play and the surprise mates 2 Qd1 and 2 Qxd4.

C

3 WALL UP THE ROOK!

> Key 1 Rb3! Waiting
> 1 ... Ke6 2 Qxe4 mate (set 2 Rxe4 mate)
> 1 ... Kd4 2 Qc3 mate
> 1 ... Kf4 2 Qg3 mate
> 1 ... Pe3 2 Qxe3 mate
> 1 ... Pf4 2 Qa1 mate

The key-move to hem in the Rook at a4 appears non-sensical, but White cannot afford to let Black play 1 ... Pb3. The Rook exists solely to pin the Black Pawn at b4 after 1 ... Kd4.

The composer is one of the Winter-Woods referred to in connection with problem *1*.

4 BURY THE BISHOP!

> Key 1 Bb1! (threat 2 Sg4 mate)
> 1 ... Rxb1 2 Pg4 mate
> 1 ... Rf4 2 Pxf4 mate
> 1 ... Rxf6 2 Qe2 mate
> 1 ... Bxb1 2 Rd5 mate
> 1 ... Be6 2 Qxa1 mate
> 1 ... Sxf6 2 Qd6 mate

Down goes the Bishop to b1, and it is a double sacrifice. No wonder the Bishop in French is 'fou' – mad! Is there method in such madness? Yes, it is a far-sighted key-move to make 2 Qxa1 possible after 1 ... Be6.

Godfrey Heathcote (1870–1952) was regarded as the patriarch of British problem chess.

5 25% CLAIMED 'NO SOLUTION'

> Key 1 Qf3! (threat 2 0–0–0 mate)
> 1 ... Kc2 2 Qe2 mate
> 1 ... Pc2 2 Ra3 mate
> 1 ... Sc4 2 Bf5 mate
> 1 ... Se4 2 Qe2 mate

Why so many solvers claimed the problem was insoluble was that in 1910 *Castling* in chess problems was widely regarded as a doubtful party trick. Solvers could not believe that the respected problem editor of 'Chess Amateur' would do such a thing.

Soon afterwards, the convention was established that Castling by White or Black is legitimate and above-board provided that King or Rook has not made an earlier move – circumstances which would disbar Castling in the game.

6 CAN/CANNOT CASTLE

Position (*a*) Try 1 Rb8? (threat 2 Be6–h3 mate)
               1 ... 0–0! 2 ?
               Key 1 Bf5! (threat 2 Rb8 mate)
               1 ... 0–0 2 Rg3 mate
Position (*b*) Try 1 Bf5? (threat 2 Rb8 mate)
               1 ... Rh3! 2 ?
               Key 1 Rb8! (threat 2 Be6–h3 mate)
               1 ... Rh3+ 2 Bxh3 mate

This two part 'twin' problem demonstrates the *Castling convention*. In the diagrammed position (*a*) Castling by Black is permissible because it cannot be proved that King or Rook has moved: the black Pawn h5 could have moved last from h7 or h6. In position (*b*), without the BPh5, it can be proved that the King or Rook moved last, and Castling to stave off mate is illegal.

7 BEGINNER'S LUCK

    Key 1 Re8! Waiting
    1 ... Kxb6 2 Bd8 mate
    1 ... Kb4 2 Bd2 mate
    1 ... Kd6 2 Bf4 mate
    1 ... Kd4 2 Bf6 mate

Even in the 1930s, the idea of the Black King fleeing to the four diagonal squares – *star-flights* – was not far short of 100 years old, but this simple problem, no more complex than its early predecessors, is worth quoting for its key-move 1 Re8! The more natural try 1 Rd8 to guard d6 and d4 is a mistake as the Rook blocks d8, and Black can play 1 ... Kxb6!

To quote Grandmaster of Composition, C. Mansfield – 'in composing bad luck seems to outweigh the good'. Fortune favoured the composer here in his first year of composition.

8 WHITE MAKES BLACK CROSS

> Key 1 Sb3! Waiting
> 1 ... Kxb3 2 Bd5 mate
> 1 ... Ka4 2 7Sc5 mate
> 1 ... Kb5 2 Bd3 mate
> 1 ... Kc4 2 Sd6 mate

Almost as old as the star-flight theme of *7* is that of *plus-flights*, a visually striking escape of the Black King to his four immediately available lateral squares. It is, however, a difficult theme for composers, and key-moves are usually less than completely satisfactory. The key to *8* is good in that it completes the cross or plus pattern, but not so good because of the need to move the Knight, and bring the Bishop and Rook (h4) into play.

9 TOO MUCH HORSE-PLAY?

> Key 1 Pf8=S! Waiting
> 1 ... bS random 2 Pc8=S mate
> 1 ... Sc8!? 2 Pxc8=S mate
> 1 ... fS random 2 Pg8=S mate
> 1 ... Sg8!? 2 Pxg8=S mate

The *promotion key* 1Pf8=S! is considered aggressive by problemists because it increases the strength of the White force and takes away a flight from the Black King – 1 ... Kxe6 is prevented – but it is in keeping with the intensive and amusing rendering of White Knight *promotion mates* and Black Knight defences. The Knights make all the running! The problem makes a strong impression, the more so when one knows the composer was blind.

10 BLACK'S TURN TO PROMOTE

Key 1 Qe8! Waiting
1 ... Kd1 2 Qh5 mate
1 ... Kf1 2 Qb5 mate
1 ... Pd1=Q 2 eSd2 mate
1 ... Pd1=S 2 Qb5 mate
1 ... Pf1=Q 2 Sf2 mate
1 ... Pf1=S 2 Qh5 mate

A similar setting but with a less good key-move was published by Charles Watney in the 'Good Companion' folder for 1920. This less well-known version avoids the unprovided check of the original setting, and has a fine retreating key 1 Qe8! to gain access to the diagonals bearing on the Black King.

The retreating key is typically problematical: a game player would as likely move in closer to the Black King!

11 CHECK AND COUNTER-CHECK

Key 1 Kg2! Waiting
1 ... Kc1 2 Bc3 mate
1 ... Bc1+ 2 Bc2 mate
1 ... Bc3+ 2 Bd2 mate
1 ... Bxd4+ 2 Bf2 mate

When a Black line-moving piece (Queen, Rook or Bishop) checks White, and White counters that check not by a capture of the Black piece but by an interposal on the check line, the result of which is mate, we have the *cross-check* theme. In Norris Easter's problem, the White King steps into three discovered checks from the Black Bishop. White's counter-checks from the Rooks are uncovered by the White Bishops, which make the right interposals at c2, d2 or f2.

12 A LOVELY PAIR!

Key 1 Kd6! (threat 2 Qb7 mate)
1 ... Kb6 2 Bc2 mate
1 ... Kb4 2 Kxc6 mate
1 ... Rg6+ 2 Be6 mate
1 ... Rd3+ 2 Bd5 mate

Probably the best *cross-check* Meredith ever made! A brilliant key grants Black two flight-squares, and exposes the White King to checks from the Black Rook. The matching pair of interferences on the Black Bishop as the Rook checks is excellent.

Gerry Anderson, a Master composer of many problem types, was the last person to play chess with that great world champion, Alexander Alekhine.

13 MUTUAL INTERFERENCE

Key 1 Qh3! (threat 2 Qd3 mate)
1 ... Re3 2 Rd4 mate
1 ... Be3 2 Qf1 mate
1 ... Se3 2 Qc8 mate
1 ... Bd4 2 Sd6 mate
1 ... Rd4 2 Rc8 mate
1 ... Se5 2 Qe6 mate

Whereas a player is pleased when the pieces support each other, a problemist is pleased when they do not! He is delighted when Black pieces can be made to trip each other up to disadvantage, and from this have grown *interference* themes. In Arthur Daniels' problem, the principal trio of interferences is at e3. The further interferences 1 ... Rd4 and 1 ... Se5 (on the Black Bishop and Rook respectively) are a neat addition.

14 WHITE TRIPS UP

Try 1 eRe2? Waiting
1 ... Pc2! 2 gRd2?
Try 1 gRe2? Waiting
1 ... fS any! 2 1Re3?
Key 1 Ra2! Waiting
1 ... Pc2 2 Ra3 mate (set 2 Rd2 mate)
1 ... fS any 2 Re3 mate
1 ... gS any 2 Se5 mate
1 ... Pg2 2 Sf2 mate

This time, White pieces interfere with White pieces! Prof. Lionel Penrose (father of many times British Chess

Champion, Dr. Jonathan Penrose) arranges for the White Rooks to seek waiting moves, but likely moves to e2 fail because the Rooks obstruct each other. The key 1 Ra2! changes the prepared mate after 1 ... Pc2.

15 ONE OVER THE EIGHT!

Key 1 Rh7! Waiting
1 ... Sxf6 2 Rg6 mate (set 2 Rg7 mate)
1 ... Sd6 2 Se7 mate
1 ... Sc5 2 Pd5 mate
1 ... Sxc3 2 Rc2 mate
1 ... Sd2 3 Rxd2 mate
1 ... Sf2 2 Rxf2 mate
1 ... Sg3 2 Rxg3 mate
1 ... Sg5 2 Rxg5 mate

Placed well away from the edge of the board, a Knight can play to a maximum of eight squares. A problemist can arrange for eight different mates after its eight moves – a *Black Knight wheel* – but a super-problemist, as Grandmaster Comins Mansfield is, can arrange nine mates, as the solution shows!

16 THOROUGHLY MODERN MÊLÉE

Key 1 Bg1! (threat 2 Qxd4 mate)
1 ... Sb5 2 Sb4 (*A*), 2 Sf4 (*B*) and 2 Qg2 (*C*) mate
1 ... Sf3 2 Sb4 (*A*) and 2 Sf4 (*B*) mate
1 ... Se6 2 Sb4 (*A*) and 2Qg2 (*C*) mate
1 ... Sc6 2 Sf4 (*B*) and 2 Qg2 (*C*) mate
1 ... Se2 2 Sb4 (*A*) mate
1 ... Sc2 2 Sf4 (*B*) mate
1 ... Sf5 2 Qg2 (*C*) mate
1 ... Sxb3 2 Qxb3 mate

This and *15* show a *Black Knight wheel* yet they make a startling contrast. Here, the composer shows every possible combination of three mates A, B and C. Near miraculously, the seven moves of the Black Knight force combinations ABC, AB, AC, BC, A, B and C – the eighth move forcing a distinct mate 2 Qxb3. This is *combinative separation*.

17 · THE QUEEN GOES FREE

> Key 1 Rh4! (threat 2 Bd4 mate)
> 1 ... Bxd5+ 2 Sxd5 mate
> 1 ... Se4 2 Qd4 mate
> 1 ... Sf3 2 Qd3 mate
> 1 ... Re4 2 Qd2 mate
> 1 ... Se6 2 Re4 mate

In a game, a pinned White Queen rarely goes free, and it is usually the end of White: in a problem, a pinned White Queen frequently goes free, and it is always the end of Black!

Black fends off the threatened 2 Bd4 mate, but *unpins* the White Queen three times by *interference*. The accurate forcing of the three Queen mates is engineered with the composer's customary elegance.

18 MITIGATING CIRCUMSTANCES

> Key 1 Be1! (threat 2 Rc5 mate)
> 1 ... Rxd6+ 2 Sxd6 mate
> 1 ... Sd3 2 Qa6 mate
> 1 ... Bd5 2 Qb4 mate
> 1 ... Sd5 2 Qc6 mate
> 1 ... Bd2 2 Qc5 mate
> 1 ... Ba3 2 Se3 mate

Black's principal defences against 2 Rc5 make the mistake of *unpinning* the White Queen by *interference* (cf.17) on the line d6–d1, and the Queen mates four times.

In spite of a normally fatal flaw of an *unprovided check* 1 ... Rxd6+ 2 ? in the diagrammed position, the problem has a place in this anthology. The composer's achievement in 1926 (very early) of forcing just one Queen mate from a potential four each time was a very real one in Meredith.

19 DIVERSIONARY TACTICS

> Key 1 Rc2! Waiting
> 1 ... Pd2 2 Rc3 mate (set 2 Rb3 mate)
> 1 ... Pxc2 2 Bc1 mate
> 1 ... eS random 2 Bc5 mate
> 1 ... Sd4!? 2 Sc4 mate
> 1 ... gS any 2 Rxe4 mate

'Mate in two' is quick, but the end would be even quicker in this problem if it were Black's turn to move. Every Black move can be answered by a mate. But it is White's turn to play, and there is no simple waiting move. The key 1 Rc2! has cunning. A new mate 2 Rc3 is provided for 1 ... Pd2, and a capture of the Rook diverts the Pawn's onward rush for 2 Bc1!, a well-concealed additional mate.

20 THE GREAT LEAP BACKWARD

> Key 1 Se3! Waiting
> 1 ... Pd3/xe3 2 Qe4 mate (set 2 Sc3 mate)
> 1 ... B any 2 Qc2 mate
> 1 ... S any 2 Qc6 mate
> 1 ... Pa5 2 Sc5 mate

This has much in common with *19*, with White seeking a waiting move to maintain set mates. Made all the more unexpected by the Knight's apparent use for mate 2 Sc3 should Black play 1 ... Pd3, is its jump back to e3! The Black Bishop's line is closed, and 2 Qe4 is a striking *changed-mate* after 1 ... Pd3. No matter if Black captures the Knight, the Pawn is diverted along the Bishop's path, and 2 Qe4 is still mate.

21 BOTH SOLUTIONS ARE RIGHT!

> *Key 1* 1 Ke6! (threat 2 Rd8 mate)
> *Key 2* 1 Pxg5 en passant! (threat 2 Rd8 mate)

If Black's last move was a King or Rook move, Castling is now illegal, and Key 1 1 Ke6! works. There is no defence against the threatened 2 Rd8 mate. If Black's last move was not a King or Rook move, it must have been a Pawn move, and that could only have been the double-jump 1 ... P(g7)–g5 (not from the occupied squares f6 and h6, or from g6 when the White King would have been in check), and Key 2 1Pxg5 en passant! (threat 2 Rd8 mate) is correct. If 1 ... 0–0 then 2 Ph7 is mate. Of course, if White attempts Key 1 Ke6?, Black Castle's out of trouble! This is a *partial analysis problem*.

22 WHY CAN'T BLACK CASTLE?

>Key 1 Qc7! (threat 2 Qf7 mate)
>1 ... Se5 2 Qe7 mate
>1 ... Sxe8 2 Qxe8 mate
>1 ... Rf8 2 Sd6 mate
>1 ... 0–0? Illegal

There is always room for a chess problem, however elementary, which makes the solver smile. Here, the composer wants the solver to believe that the key 1 Qc7! (which apparently lets Black Castle with the guard on f8 abandoned) cannot be right because when Black makes the Castling move White is unable to mate. But look at that Black Rook on h7. How did it get there? The answer is only via h8, and in doing so it must have displaced the existing Black Rook on h8 (or it is the original Black Rook from h8), and Black has clearly lost the right to Castle. 1 Qc7! is correct!

23 FORCE THE PACE

>Key 1 Rb4! (threat 2 Rb5 mate)
>1 ... Bg2 2 Sg4 mate
>1 ... Sb3/e4 2 Re4 mate
>1 ... Sd3 2 Sxd3 mate

Difficult to solve. The solver is reluctant to abandon the mates which are provided for all the Black moves in the diagrammed position – Black is in *Zugzwang*. The mates are 1 ... Bxg4 2 Sxg4, 1 ... Bg2/f1 2 Rg5, 1 ... dS any 2 Re4, and 1 ... eS any 2 Sd3. Almost always a waiting move would solve such problems, but *23* demands a threat. 1 Rb4! is a nicely determined key (1 Ra4? fails to 1 ... Sc4!), and the Black pieces make specific defences rather than aimless moves.

24 ATTACK IS BEST FORM OF DEFENCE

Key 1 Qc8! (threat 2 Qxa8 mate)
1 ... Kd5 2 Qxa8 mate
1 ... Kf3 2 Qf5 mate
1 ... Bb7/c6 2 Qxb7/xc6 mate
1 ... Bd5 2 Qf5 mate
1 ... Sg4 2 Bg2 mate

Like *23*, this is a tricky *block-threat* problem, but then the famous Warton brothers, Thomas and Joseph, never made anything other than tricky problems. Their speciality was the three-mover, and such was the difficulty of some of their work that despairing letters came from far and wide begging chess editors to give the solutions! There is no waiting move to solve this problem: only a flight-giving 1 Qc8! to threaten 2 Qxa8 mate is the answer.

25 KINGPIN

Key 1 Kd8! Waiting
1 ... R moves (including Rd3+) 2 Bd5 mate
1 ... Sc2 2 Bd5 mate
1 ... B any 2 Qxc3 mate
1 ... Pa3 2 Qb5 mate

In some problems – *22* for example – the White King has no function on the board other than to comply with the convention that he must be there, but it is certainly not the case here. Without the White King, there is no problem! A waiting move to solve the problem can come only from the White King, and only 1 Kd8! prevents the Queen or Bishop from becoming pinned e.g. 1Kd6? Ba3! 2 Qxc3? 1 Kc6/7/8? Pa3! 2 Qb5?, and 1 Ke6/7/8? Re3! 2 Bd5?

26 THE POWER BEHIND THE THRONE

> Key 1 Qg7! Waiting
> 1 ... Pc5 2 Qb7 mate
> 1 ... Pe5 2 Qf7 mate
> 1 ... Pf5 2 Qd4 mate
> 1 ... Pe3 2 Qg2 mate

Again, the White King makes this witty problem, but it is no more than a well-meaning nuisance. It is the White Queen which emerges as the strong person!

The reasoning behind possible first moves by the White King – 1 Kf7? Pe5! 2 Qg8? 1 Kg7? Pf5! 2 Qd4? and 1 Kh7? Pe3! 2 Qh1? – is to clear the rank for 2 Qa8 mate after the square vacating 1 ... Pc5, but the White King always manages to obstruct the Queen. 1 Qg7! provides a new mate 2 Qb7 after 1 ... Pc5, and changed mates after 1 ... Pe5 and 1 ... Pe3.

27 KING KEY

> Key 1 Kh6! (threat 2 Ra5 mate)
> 1 ... Rxb6+ 2 Kxb6 mate
> 1 ... Bd6 2 Qxg1 mate
> 1 ... Bc6/Rh5 2 Qa5 mate
> 1 ... Bb7+ 2 Kxb7 mate
> 1 ... Rg5 2 Rb1 mate

Problems with the White King discovering checkmate are fascinating because they pose situations which rarely happen in a game. The White King marches into a pin of the White Queen (a suicidal game manoeuvre!) and two checks from Black. But the odds are fixed in White's favour. Two of the six mates are discovered check-mates by the White King, and two are mates by the unpinned Queen.

28 FLEDG-LING!

> Key 1 Qc5! (threat 2 Qa5 mate)
> 1 ... Qb6 2 Qxb6 mate
> 1 ... Qb5+/c7 2 Qb5 mate
> 1 ... Qc6+ 2 Qxc6 mate
> 1 ... Qb4+ 2 Kxb4 mate
> 1 ... Qb3+ 2 Kxb3 mate

It hardly seems credible that a release of the Black Queen should be the quickest way of check-mating Black. The White King looks far too vulnerable. However, it is the exposed White King, in the K+R battery combination of *27*, which plays a vital role by making two discovered mate captures of the Black Queen.

This pleasing problem was John Ling's *first composition* at the age of 15!

29 TOP RANK ENTERTAINMENT!

> Key 1 Bg5! (threat 2 Qd8 mate)
> 1 ... 0–0+ 2 Bd8 mate
> 1 ... Kf8 2 Qxh8 mate
> 1 ... Bd7 2 Qxh8 mate

1 Bg5! seems such a crazy key-move that, at first sight, White appears to have lost the will to win. The White Rook is shut off from a position of strength, and Black is allowed to Castle with check! But the prodigal Bishop returns to d8 with a counter-check from the Rook, and Black finds that he has Castled not to safety but into mate. It is worth noting the tries 1 Bf6? Kf8! and 1 Bh4? Rxh4!

30 MATED IN THE BACK ROW

> Key 1 Rf5! Waiting
> 1 ... Kh7+ 2 Rf8 mate
> 1 ... Rh7 2 Rb8 mate
> 1 ... Pg6/5 2 Bc4 mate
> 1 ... B any 2 Rxg7 mate

As in *29*, the Black King discovers check on the top rank – or Black's back row – but this time it is a White Rook masking a Bishop, and not a Bishop masking a Rook which makes the *cross-check*.

The problem, entered in a competition for British

composers under 21, is most elegantly constructed. The key-move, giving the Black King a flight-square at h7, is first-class. Try 1 Rf4? Bxf4!

31 OUT OF CONTROL

> Key 1 Sf4! (threat 2 Qe8 mate)
> 1 ... Qa3 2 Ra5 mate
> 1 ... Qb2 2 Rb5 mate
> 1 ... Qc3 2 Rc5 mate
> 1 ... Qxd5 2 Bxc2 mate
> 1 ... Qxe3/a4 2 Qa4 mate

To guard against 2 Qe8 and the *secondary threat* of 2 Bxc2 mate (if 1 ... Qb8 2 Bxc2 mate, for example) the Queen is drawn to a3, b2 and c3 where her initial dual control of the Q+R battery is lost, and shut-off mates 2 Ra5, 2 Rb5 and 2 Rc5 follow.

The composer's art is revealed by the use made of the White Queen. A Bishop at a8 would be sufficient for the trio of battery mates, but a Queen admits an elegant threat 2 Qe8 as well as a pin-mate 2 Qa3 after 1 ... Qxe3.

32 ON HIS MAJESTY'S SERVICE

> Key 1 Ke5! (threat 2 Rc8 mate)
> 1 ... Qxe4+ 2 Bxe4 mate
> 1 ... Qb2+ 2 Sc3 mate
> 1 ... Qb5+ 2 Sc5 mate
> 1 ... Qb8+ 2 Sd6 mate
> 1 ... Qb7 2 Qc5 mate
> 1 ... Qb6 2 Qd7 mate
> 1 ... Sd6 2 Rxd6 mate

Scornful of the Black Queen, the White King shows the way by advancing on the Black King to add a guard on d5 for a threatened 2 Rc8 mate. Piqued, the Black Queen checks at b2, b5 and b8, but the King's trusty Knight closes the check lines three times with a counter-check and mate (*cross-checks*) from the now unguarded White Bishop.

33 TAKES TWO TO TANGLE

> Key 1 Rd3! Waiting
> 1 ... Rd2 2 Re3 mate
> 1 ... Rxd3 2 Sxd3 mate
> 1 ... R else 2 Rxd5 mate
> 1 ... Bd2 2 Rxd5 mate (set 2 Sd3 mate)
> 1 ... Be3 2 Rxe3 mate
> 1 ... Bxf4 2 Qe7 mate (set 2 Qxf4 mate)
> 1 ... Pd4 2 Qxd4 mate (set 2 Qe7 mate)
> 1 ... S any 2 Sg6 mate

Mates are prepared for every Black move, including the distinctive *mutual interference pair* 1 ... Rd2 and 1 ... Bd2 (a classic 'tangle' which will be seen in many problems in this book), but there is no simple waiting move – for example, a White Pawn at a4 would solve the problem by 1 Pa5! The key 1 Rd3! *changes* three of the set mates.

34 GRIMSHAW

> Key 1 Qe3! Waiting
> 1 ... Ke1 2 Qg1 mate
> 1 ... Kc2 2 Qb3 mate
> 1 ... Rb2 2 Qc1 mate
> 1 ... Bb2 2 Qd2 mate
> 1 ... Rc2 2 Qg1 mate
> 1 ... Rd2 2 Qxd2 mate
> 1 ... Rxe2 2 Qxe2 mate

Mutual interference between Black Rook and Bishop – a *Grimshaw* – is derived from a British composer, Walter Grimshaw (1832–1890), and has been shown so many times that the risk for composers of having their problems already shown by others – '*anticipated*' – is great. Don Smedley struck lucky with the charming *34*. The Grimshaw at b2 is enhanced by a fine key-move which gives two flights.

35 TWEEDLEDUM AND TWEEDLEDEE

> Key 1 Qh1! (threat 2 Qc6 mate)
> 1 ... Be4 2 Qh2 mate
> 1 ... Re4 2 Qh7 mate
> 1 ... Bb5 2 Qb7 mate
> 1 ... Rb5 2 Sa6 mate
> 1 ... Rb6 2 Pxb6 mate

Which is which of the quarrelsome pair, the Black Rook or Bishop, is impossible to say, but that they cannot agree is not in doubt. They obstruct each other at e4, and then they do it again at b5.

This is the *Grimshaw* of *33* and *34 doubled* with just one pair of pieces, and represents an excellent achievement in Meredith form.

36 FOUR HANDS ROUND

> Try 1 Qb6? (threat 2 Qe3 mate)
> 1 ... Rd4 2 Qxe6 mate
> 1 ... Bd4 2 Qb1 mate
> 1 ... Rd3 2 Rf4 mate
> 1 ... Bd2! 2 ?
> Key 1 Qc7! (threat 2 Qf4 mate)
> 1 ... Re5 2 Sf6 mate
> 1 ... Be5 2 Qh7 mate
> 1 ... Rf5 2 Re3 mate

The double Grimshaw by the Black Rook and Bishop in *35* has a jargon name of *Four Hands Round* theme – a baffling tag. It has nothing to do with this composer's trying his *hand* – in a remarkable *first problem* – at a modern try-play setting with *hand*some results!

37 CORRECTIVE MEASURES

> Key 1 Qa8! (threat 2 Qd8 mate)
> 1 ... B random 2 Qxf8 mate
> 1 ... Bf7!? 2 hSf5 mate
> 1 ... R random on file 2 Qxe8 mate
> 1 ... Rf7!? 2 Sg6 mate
> 1 ... Bg6+ 2 Sxg6 mate

The *Grimshaw* interferences (cf.34) at f7 are for a new reason. 1 ... B random (xh5) stops the threatened 2 Qd8 by letting through the Rook's guard, but then White can play 2 Qxf8 mate. The improved move or *correction* 1 ... Bf7!? prevents both 2 Qd8 and 2 Qxf8 (the White Rook's line is closed), but the Black Rook is interfered with, and 2 hSf5 is mate. 1 ... Rf7!? 2 Sg6 mate is by a similar process of *correction* to complete the Grimshaw.

38 NEW MATES FOR OLD?

> Key 1 Pg7! (threat 2 Qh5 mate)
> 1 ... Rf7 2 Pg8=S mate (set 2 Sg8 mate)
> 1 ... Bf7 2 Pxf8=Q mate (set 2 Qxf8 mate)
> 1 ... Sg6+ 2 Qxg6 mate

After experience of the previous *Grimshaw* problem and related examples, the solver's attention is likely to be drawn to the f7 cutting point of the Black Rook (d7) and Bishop: they cut each other's line to let in 2 Sg8 mate and 2 Qxf8 mate. The key-move destroys these mates, and the new ones are 2 Pg8=S and 2 Pxf8=Q. The new mates are on the same squares g8 and f8, and are again by Knight and Queen – but not the same Knight and Queen! It is a very subtle change.

39 A LOW-DOWN DIVE

> Key 1 Qh1! (threat 2 Bb7 mate)
> 1 ... Pxb4 2 Bf1 mate
> 1 ... Pd5 2 Sxc5 mate
> 1 ... Ra7/b8 2 Sb8 mate

The two-move problem is the problemist's laboratory. Experiments are made with the latent powers of the pieces, and new ideas are set out in elemental form. The dive into the corner 1 Qh1! solves this problem, but the element of real interest is the *support* of the minor piece, the Bishop (g2), by the major piece, the Queen. The support is direct in the threat line 2 Bb7, and indirect after 1 ... Pxb4 2 Bf1 mate when the Queen continues to hold b7.

This simple *support* idea is still a source of inspiration.

40 ... DIVIDED WE FALL

    Key 1 1 Qxc5! Waiting
                1 ... Kxd6 2 Qc6 mate
                1 ... Pc3 2 Qf2 mate
    Key 2 1 Qxc4! Waiting
                1 ... Kxd5 2 Qd4 mate
                1 ... Pxb4 2 Qf1 mate

The Queen *supports* a minor piece in *39*, but here the role is reversed. By capturing at c5 and c4, the Queen clears the lines of the Rook and Bishop which are then able to give their indirect support to the Queen in the mates.

The *second solution* is not a *cook* as might be inferred from the 'Hints for Solving'. The second solution is intentional because the two pairs of mates are meaningless in isolation.

41 WHAT GOES UP ...

                Key 1 Pe4! Waiting
                1 ... S random 2 Qa5 mate
                1 ... Sd2!? 2 Re3 mate
                1 ... Pc4 2 Qe3 mate
                1 ... Pxf2 2 hRe3 mate
                1 ... Ph1=Q+ 2 Rxh1 mate

Up two squares goes the White Pawn, but it has no aspirations of promotion. It is a *clearance* move for the Queen and Rooks to mate at e3.

In *143* and *144*, you will see different types of clearance moves by pieces which still have a further part to play in the solution, but 1 Pe4! is a clearance move pure and simple.

Almost an exception to 'what goes up, must come down' is the Pawn. It comes down only as a promoted piece!

42 ... MUST COME DOWN!

>Key 1 Qh1! Waiting
>1 ... Kxg6 2 Qh7 mate
>1 ...Rf4+ 2 Qe4 mate (set 2 Rxf4 mate)
>1 ... Pg4 2 Qh5 mate
>1 ... S any 2 Qb1 mate (set 2 Rxf3 mate)

Perhaps the caption, with that of *41*, is too strong a clue to the key-move? This time, a Queen drops to the relative obscurity of h1. If the solver sees the mates 2 Rxf4 and 2 Rxf3 prepared for 1 ... Rf4+ and 1 ... S any in the diagrammed position, the surprise of the key-move – especially as it gives the Black King a flight-square at g6 – is even greater. A successful *changed-mate* problem!

43 CAT AND MOUSE SITUATION

>Key 1 Kd7! (threat 2 Qc5 mate)
>1 ... Kf5 2 Kd6 mate
>1 ... Kd4 2 Ke6 mate
>1 ... Pf5 2 Qc3 mate

In the diagrammed position, the Black King is tightly held at e5 by the raking effect of the White pieces. Unexpectedly, the White King loosens the hold by a move to d7 which closes the lines of the Queen and Rook, and the Black King scuttles to f5 and d4. The White King dabs out 2 Kd5 and 2 Ke6, and the Black King is caught again with the finality of mate.

44 TOP CAT AND MOUSE SITUATION!

>Key 1 Sa3+!
>1 ... Ka4 2 Kb2 mate (set 2 Kc3 mate)
>1 ... Kc5 2 Kd3 mate (set 2 Kb3 mate)
>1 ... Kxa3 2 Ra1 mate

Yes, this problem tops the play of *43!* The Black King can run to a4 and c5 in the diagrammed position, but the White King merely reaches out 2 Kc3 and 2 Kb3

mate. A *checking key-move* 1 Sa3+! pats the Black
King to a4 and c5 again, but the White King then delights
in pouncing in a new way 2 Kb2 and 2 Kd3 mate to show
his absolute superiority.

You will read in chess problem text-books that checking key-moves are considered inartistic. In most cases,
this is true. Only real artists can ignore convention success-
fully as in *44*.

45 UP THE JUNCTION!

> Key 1 Be6! (threats 2 Sd5, 2 Se2 and 2 Rd3
> mate)
> 1 ... Rxe6 2 Sd5 mate
> 1 ... Bxe6 2 Se2 mate
> 1 ... Bg6+ 2 Rd3 mate

When Black Rook and Bishop trip over each other
at a junction point, it is the Grimshaw theme explained
in *34*. When White takes the initiative by playing to a
junction point (usually to threaten two mates as a result
of the Black Rook and Bishop being interfered with), it is
the *Nowotny* theme. Captures by Rook and Bishop
separate threatened mates

46 WHITE MAKES CUTTING POINTS

> Try 1 Be5? (threats 2 Sg7 and 2 Re7 mate)
> 1 ... Rxe5 2 Sg7 mate
> 1 ... Bxe5 2 Rd7 mate
> 1 ... Sxh7! 2 ?
> Try 1 Rd4? (threats 2 Sf6 and 2 Sd6 mate)
> 1 ... Rxd4 2 Sf6 mate
> 1 ... Bxd4 2 Sd6 mate
> 1 ... Se4 2 Re7 mate
> 1 ... Re6! 2 ?
> Try 1 Sd4? (threats 2 Sf6 and 2 Rd8 mate)
> 1 ... Rxd4 2 Sf6 mate
> 1 ... Bxd4 2 Rd8 mate
> 1 ... Re7! 2 ?

Key 1 Bd4! (threats 2 Sg7 and 2 Rd8 mate)
1 ... Rxd4 2 Sg7 mate
1 ... Bxd4 2 Rd8 mate
1 ... Se6 2 Re7 mate

See *45*: this problem is probably the most complex *multiple Nowotny* ever made with so few pieces.

47 LONG RANGE INTERFERENCE

Key 1 dRd1! (threat 2 bRc1 mate)
1 ... Re6 2 Qc8 mate
1 ... Be6 2 Qf2 mate
1 ... Se6 2 Qxf5 mate
1 ... Pd5 2 Qc5 mate

In *13* it was shown that Black Rook, Bishop and Knight moves to the same square can be engineered by the composer to Black's disadvantage. Here, the three moves to e6 are to close the White Bishop's line of guard to b3, and to keep the threatening White Rook tied to that square – but it is Black who gets tied up!

A splendid feature of this problem (and desirable in all problems) is the *try* 1 Pb4? to threaten 2 Bb3 mate. The try induces the same interferences at e6 and the same mates, but fails only to 1 ... Bd3!

48 FORECLOSURES

Key 1 Se5! (threat 2 Sc4 mate)
1 ... Rf5 2 Rd7 mate
1 ... Bf5 2 Sf7 mate
1 ... Sf5 2 Rg6 mate

Again, the Black Rook, Bishop and Knight interference trio, but the motivation for the three moves to f5 is different. The threatened 2 Sc4 mate would close the Bishop's line to d5, but open the Rook's. Black plays to f5 as a *prospective unguard* of d5! Now, if 2 Sc4? Kxd5! But Black is in the usual tangle.

49 PERCY BLAKE? SEXTON BLAKE!

Key 1 Qa1! Waiting
1 ... Kd4 2 Qa7 mate
1 ... Pd4 2 Qxc1 mate
1 ... Pe4 2 Sf5 mate
1 ... Sa4 or d1 2 Qxe5 mate (set 2 Qd3 mate)
1 ... Sc4 2 Qc3 mate
1 ... Sd3 2 Sxd5 mate

The help of the great detective (or knowledgeable solvers!) is wanted to solve two mysteries relating to this and *50*. What was the date of publication of *49*? Where and when was *50* first published? These facts are well worth establishing as Percy Blake (1873–1936) was one of Britain's and world's greatest composers.

50 IN THE OLD-FASHIONED WAY

Key 1 Qb2! Waiting
1 ... Kc5 2 Se4 mate
1 ... Bb6 2 Qxb6 mate
1 ... Bc5 2 Sc6 mate
1 ... cB any 2 Qf2 mate
1 ... Be4+ 2 Sd5 mate
1 ... Pe4 2 Sa4 mate
1 ... Sc4 2 Se6 mate
1 ... S else 2 Qb4 mate

The problem has a passable key-move, and a nice collection of mates. This was the style before the turn of the century: today, there needs to be a pointed theme, something by which a problem can be easily labelled. Do you see the basic resemblance of Mrs. Baird's *1* to this composition?

51 A 17 YEAR OLD DOYEN!

Key 1 Qf8! Waiting
1 ... Kxe5 2 Pd4 mate
1 ... Rb5 2 Sxc6 mate
1 ... Bb5 2 Qd6 mate

1 ... Rc5 2 Qf4 mate
1 ... Rd5 2 Sf3 mate
1 ... Rxe5 2 Qb4 mate
1 ... B else 2 Sxc6 mate

Guy Chandler was 17 when he made this pleasing affair with three square blockings by the Black Rook and a *Grimshaw* (cf.*34*) at b5. He is 87 now, and is still composing. In a lifetime's devotion to problem chess, he has been the mainstay of the *British Chess Problem Society*. He was the mentor of our first Grandmaster, Comins Mansfield MBE, with whom he became friends in 1912.

52 THE DISAPPEARING TRICK

Key 1 Bd3! (threats 2 Qe4 and 2 Qe3 mate)
1 ... Kxd3 2 Ke7 mate
1 ... Rxd3 2 Qg4 mate
1 ... Bxd3 2 Be3 mate
1 ... Re8 2 Kxc6 mate

Like *51*, this problem was the work of a composer in his 'teens. What is so curious about this excellent *Nowotny* problem (cf. *45* and *46*) is that the standard double-threat created by White's move 1 Bd3! to the Rook and Bishop's junction point is not separated by Rook and Bishop captures – but eliminated by them. The blocks at d3 cause new mates 2 Qg4 and 2 Be3. Fine use is made of the White King which delivers two discovered check-mates.

53 SIGNS OF INTELLIGENCE

Key 1 Sd4! Waiting
1 ... Kxd4 2 Qd5 mate
1 ... dR random 2 Qd5 mate
1 ... Rxd4!? 2 Qg6 mate
1 ... hR random 2 Qg4 mate
1 ... Rf4!? 2 Qd5 mate
1 ... B random 2 Qxh4 or 2 Qe3 mate
1 ... Bxd4!? 2 Sxd6 mate
1 ... Pd5 2 Qe5 mate

If *53* were a game, and you touched the Black Rook
(d2), you would soon realise to your dismay that the
mere fact of moving the Rook (as you would have to)
would permit White to mate you by 2 Qd5. 1 ... Rxd4
would seem to save the situation, but the blocking of
square d4 lets in a new mate 2 Qg6. Black *corrects* the
mistake of a move *at random – Black correction.*

54　INTUITIVE BEGINNINGS

> Key 1 Qa5! Waiting
> 1 ... Kc3 2 Re2 mate
> 1 ... 6S random 2 Qxb4 mate
> 1 ... 6Sd5!? 2 Re4 mate
> 1 ... Sc4!? 2 Sb5 mate
> 1 ... 4S random 2 Qd2 mate
> 1 ... Sd3!? 2 Pc3 mate

Thomas Taverner (1856–1928) was one of the best
British composers, and his problem, like *53*, pre-dates
the 1930s' vogue for *Black correction,* the fanciful attribu-
tion to Black of being able to improve on a random move
not properly thought out.

55　WHAT A RELIEF!

> Key 1 Kg7! Waiting
> 1 ... Rf7+ 2 Kxf7 mate
> 1 ... Rf8 2 Kxf8 mate
> 1 ... Rg6+ 2 Kxg6 mate
> 1 ... Rh6 2 Kxh6 mate
> 1 ... Re6 2 Rd5 mate
> 1 ... Rxd6 2 Re1 mate
> 1 ... Rf5 2 Sg6 mate
> 1 ... Rf4 2 Qd5 mate

A bold move of the White King is needed to unpin
the Rook, and to relieve a *stalemate* position. Suddenly,

Black has eight moves, but the Rook's freedom is short-lived. A different mate is arranged for each of them.

56 THE LONE RANGER

> (a) Key 1 Sd2! Kd4 2 Qe4 mate
> (b) Key 1 Bd5! Kxd5 2 Qf5 mate
> (c) Key 1 Pc6! Kxd6 2 Bc7 mate
> (d) Key 1 Be6! Kxe6 2 Qe4 mate
> (e) Key 1 Qf1! Ke4 2 Qf4 mate
> (f) Key 1 Pg4! Kf4 2 Qf5 mate
> (g) Key 1 Ba5! Kxf6 2 Bc3 mate
> (h) Key 1 Qh1! Kf5 2 Qd5 mate

Again, relief of *stalemate* is the theme, but it gets a most distinctive and intensive treatment from our Grandmaster composer. The eight different placings of the White King determine which of the eight key-moves to relieve stalemate is correct. Amusingly, the lone Black King ranges to each of its adjacent eight squares in the full course of the eight solutions.

57 CLASSIC FOCAL PLAY

> Key 1 Qa6! Waiting
> 1 ... R moves 2 Qe2 or 2 Qg6 mate
> (set 2 1Sd2 or 2 Sg3 mate)
> 1 ... Pd3 2 Qe6 mate (set 2 Qe7 mate)

In the diagrammed position, moves of the Black Rook result in a fatal loss of control of either g3 or d2. In problem terminology, the Black Rook loses its *focal control*, and mates 2 Sg3 or 2 1Sd2 result.

The key-move destroys the set mates (by leaving the Knight tied to e3), and imposes new focal duties on the Black Rook. Now, its moves result in loss of control of e2 or g6, and mates 2 Qe2 or 2 Qg6 follow. This is *the* text-book example of focal play.

58 BREAK THE BISHOP'S GRIP

> Try 1 Sd4? Waiting
> 1 ... B moves 2 Sc6 or 2 dSb3 mate
> 1 ... Bb7! 2 dSb3? Kb4/5/6!
> Try 1 Sd6? Waiting
> 1 ... B moves 2 dSb7 or 2 Sc4 mate
> 1 ... Bb3! 2 dSb7? Kb4/5/6!
> Key 1 Sc3! Waiting
> 1 ... B moves 2 Sb7 or 2 Sb3 mate

Again, this is the *focal theme* of 57, but in modern guise. Each try by the Knight sets up two potential mates, one of which will result when the Black Bishop moves, and loses its focal hold. The tries are most ingeniously refuted, but the Bishop's grip is finally broken by 1 Sc3!

59 VICE VERSA

> Key 1 Qb6! (threat 2 Qe6 mate)
> 1 ... Kxf5 2 Rxd5 mate (set 2 Rxe3 mate)
> 1 ... Ke4 2 Rxe3 mate (set 2 Rxd5 mate)

An examination of Black King moves in the diagrammed position almost always provides a clue to a problem's solution. Here, two moves 1 ... Kxf5 and 1 ... Ke4 result in mates 2 Rxe3 and 2 Rxd5 respectively, and it becomes apparent that to give mate on the second move the White Queen will be needed to control the awkward square combination of e4, e5 and f5. After the key-move 1 Qb6! the Black King makes his two moves as defences against the threatened 2 Qe6 mate, but it is not the previously seen mates 2 Rxe3 and 2 Rxd5 which occur, but a vice versa sequence 2 Rxd5 and 2 Rxe3 mate! This is *reciprocal change*.

60 ABBA

> Key 1 Qxc6! Waiting
> 1 ... Kxa6 2 Ra8 mate
> 1 ... Q random (xe1) 2 Qb5 mate – *A*

1 ... Qb4!? 2 Ra1 mate　　　　− *B*
1 ... B random (d8) 2 Ra1 mate　− *B*
1 ... Bc5!? 2 Qb5 mate　　　　− *A*
1 ... S any 2 Bxc3 mate

The vice versa effect of the mating moves of *59* is seen again here, but in a quite different form. The random and correction moves (cf.53) of the Black Queen and Bishop form an *ABBA pattern* when tabulated. The mate for the random moves of one piece is the mate for the correction move of another piece – and vice versa. Problemists call this *reciprocal correction*.

61 A PAWN IN THE GAME

　　　Key 1 Qd8! Waiting
　　　1 ... Kd6 2 Qxe7 mate
　　　1 ... Pxc6 2 Qxe7 mate
　　　1 ... Pd6 2 Bd4 mate
　　　1 ... Pd5 2 Qxd5 mate
　　　1 ... Pxe6 2 Qd4 mate

The Black Pawn has humble origins at square d7, but the composer's art makes it no 'mere' Pawn. Its Herculean efforts of a maximum of four moves make it the centre of attraction, and it is the Black Pawn's activity which is the memorable feature rather than the four different mates by White it forces.

62 PICKANINNY

　　　Key 1 Sf6! Waiting
　　　1 ... Ke6/e5 2 Qd5 mate
　　　1 ... Kxg5 2 Qxf4 mate
　　　1 ... Pxf6 2 Rc5 mate
　　　1 ... Pe6 2 Qxf4 mate
　　　1 ... Pe5 2 Qg4 mate
　　　1 ... Pxd6 2 Qd5 mate

Kindly meant when this type of problem was labelled some fifty years ago is the tag *Pickaninny*. It was meant to be a graphic summing up of the four eye-catching moves of the baby Black Pawn, and the name has stuck.

1 Sf6! is fine key-move to this example. It sacrifices the Knight, gives the Black King a third flight-square at g5, and, most important, gives the Black Pawn at e7 its fourth move, 1 ... Pxf6.

63 TOP OF THE FORM

>   Key 1 Se3! Waiting
>   1 ... Qg3 2 Qf6 mate
>   1 ... Qf3 2 Sd3 mate
>   1 ... Qxe3 2 Rxf7 mate
>   1 ... Q else 2 Sg2 or 2 Qg4 mate
>   1 ... Pd4 2 Re4 mate
>   1 ... Pc5 2 Sxd5 mate
>   1 ... S any 2 Qe5 mate

Most problems are judged successful if Black moves result in one mate only. It is the notable feature of *63* that as many as 15 moves of the Black Queen each permits only one mate e.g. 1 ... Qh6 pins the White Queen, and only 2 Sg2 is possible. Had White been left with a choice of mates after any Black Queen move, the problem would have been *dualised* and spoilt. However, full marks for accuracy!

64 BATTLE ROYAL

>   Key 1 Bf6! Waiting
>   1 ... Qg4 2 Qb8 mate
>   1 ... Q else 2 Qg5 or 2 Qg3 mate
>   1 ... Pe3 2 Qb4 mate

In similar vein to *63*, this problem makes a feature of *accurate play* after Black Queen moves. 1 Bf6! limits the Black Queen to nine squares, and the scene is set for the struggle of their majesties. White Queen mates 2 Qg5 or 2 Qg3 (but never both) follow the Black Queen's moves. 1 ... Qg4 stops mates at g5 and g3, but g4 is blocked, and the White Queen swings off to mate at a8.

A good touch to make even fuller use of the White Queen is the variation 1 ... Pe3 2 Qb4.

65 DON'T ALL RUSH

> Key 1 Pxb7! (threats 2 Pxa8=Q,
>   2 Pb8=S, 2 Pxc8= Q and 2 Bb5 mate)
> 1 ... Bd7 2 Pxa8=Q mate
> 1 ... Sb6 2 Pb8=S mate
> 1 ... Sc7 2 Pxc8=Q mate
> 1 ... Bxb7 2 Bb5 mate

The fiercely attacking move 1 Pxb7! threatens a rush of four mates – yet the composer has arranged the pieces so that each Black move eliminates three of the threats, and only one mate is possible at a time. The problem is a remarkably early example of *threat separation*.

66 LEGAL SEPARATION

> Key 1 Se7! (threats 2 Qd5, 2 Qf5,
>   2 Qg4 and 2 Qe2 mate)
> 1 ... Bxf6 2 Qd5 mate
> 1 ... Bxg3 2 Qf5 mate
> 1 ... Sxg3 2 Qg4 mate
> 1 ... Sxf2 2 Qe2 mate
> 1 ... Bg5 2 Qxh1 mate

65 achieved the *separation of four threatened mates* neatly enough. The Grandmaster touch reduces 12 pieces to 9, devises a far from obvious key-move, and adds a *fifth mate*, 2. Qxh1. This fifth mate is important to problemists who revel in the technicalities of 1 ... Bg5 eliminating four threatened mates in favour of 2 Qxh1. It is worth setting up the pieces to find out why.

67 CURIOUSER AND CURIOUSER

> Key 1 Sf2! (threat 2 Qxe4 mate)
> 1 ... Ke6 2 Qxf5 mate
> 1 ... Kc4 2 Qxd3 mate
> 1 ... Qe5 2 Qf7 mate
> 1 ... Rd4 2 Qb3 mate

'White cannot mate Black until he can unpin Black' – you might think that the unpinned man would then be free to frustrate the mate – is not the paradox it sounds. The pinned Queen and d-Rook are induced to e5 and d4 where, still pinned, they interfere with the e-Rook's paths to e6 and c4, defences which would otherwise prevent unpinning moves 2 Qf7 and 2 Qb3 from mating. Curious.

Problemists call this strategy a *Gamage unpin*.

68 *GOETHART UNPINS*

        Try 1 Bd1? Waiting
        1 ... S random 2 Rxa7 mate
        1 ... Sb6!? 2 Sa4 mate (2 ... Bf2?)
        1 ... Pb3! 2 ?
        Key 1 Sd1! Waiting
        1 ... S random 2 Rxa7 mate
        1 ... Sb6!? 2 Ba4 mate (2 ... Bf2?)
        1 ... Pb3 2 Sc3 mate

White is obliged to wait for the line-closing 1 ... Sb6 in try and post-key play before unpinning moves 2 Sa4 and 2 Ba4 to mate Black are possible. It is another interpretation of the 'White unpins Black' idea of *67*.

This is a *Goethart unpin*, and differs from the Gamage unpin (cf.*67*) because here it is the firing piece of a battery which unpins Black.

69 *PASSED OVER PAWN*

        Key 1 Rb5! Waiting
        1 ... Pxb1=Q 2 Ra5 mate
        1 ... Pxb1=S 2 Kb4 mate
        1 ... Pc1=Q 2 Kc5 mate
        1 ... Pc1=S 2 Rxd2 mate
        1 ... Rd4+ 2 Kxd4 mate

10 shows four *promotions* by two Black Pawns, but this shows four promotions by a single Black Pawn. Note how the Black Rook is pinned and unable to capture the Bishop of the B+K battery when the Pawn promotes.

How galling it would be in a game to have this passed Pawn!

70 SAME BUT DIFFERENT!

Key 1 Sf5! (threats 2 Sd6 (*A*),
   2 Sg3 (*B*) and 2 Qd4 (*C*) mate)
1 ... Pg1=S 2 Sd6 (*A*), 2 Sg3 (*B*) and 2 Qd4 (*C*) mate
1 ... Pg1=B 2 Sd6 (*A*) and 2 Sg3 (*B*) mate
1 ... Pg1=R 2 Sd6 (*A*) and 2 Qd4 (*C*) mate
1 ... Sc8 2 Sg3 (*B*) and 2 Qd4 (*C*) mate
1 ... Pg1=Q 2 Sd6 (*A*) mate
1 ... Sb5 2 Sg3 (*B*) mate
1 ... Bxf7 2 Qd4 (*C*) mate

Whereas 69 showed one Black Pawn making four *promotions* on two squares, the Black Pawn here makes four promotions on the same square! There is similarity, but the difference is astounding. White threatens three mates 2 Sd6, 2 Sg3 and 2 Qd4 which are labelled A, B and C. All possible promotions to Queen, Rook, Bishop and Knight serve only to force different combinations of A, B and C. Other Black moves complete the mathematical pattern of *combinative separation*.

71 TWO UNPINS OF A BISHOP

Key 1 Qg8! (threat 2 Qe8 mate)
1 ... Sc5 2 Bc6 mate
1 ... Se5 2 Bb3 mate
1 ... Sb4 2 Sc3 mate
1 ... Rxa8 2 Qxa8 mate
1 ... Ra7/a6 2 Rxa7xa6 mate

The composer sets the scene for *Black unpins White* in fine style by having the Queen key-move leave the Bishop pinned by the Black Rook, itself pinned by the

White Rook. Knight moves 1 ... Sc5 and 1 ... Se5 to stop the threatened 2 Qe8 mate make the mistake of *unpinning* the Bishop by *interference* on the Black Rook's pin-line, and two neatly separated mates 2 Bc6 and 2 Bb3 result.

72 GRANDMASTER CLASS

> Key 1Qe2! (threat 2 Qxe7 mate)
> 1 ... Kd7 2 Qxe7 mate
> 1 ... S random 2 Qb5 mate
> 1 ... Sd3!? 2 Bc6 mate
> 1 ... Sd7!? 2 Bf7 mate
> 1 ... P any 2 Rxd8 mate

1Qe2! gives the Black King a flight-square at d7, and that really is a fine touch. Then there is the refinement of Black being able simply to lift the Knight at c5 to stop the threatened 2 Qxe7 by letting through the Black Bishop – but the mistake is to let in 2 Qb5 mate. 1 ... Sd3!? blocks the Queen's path, but *unpins* the Bishop for 2 Bc6 mate. 1 ... Se7!? is another move to stop 2 Qg5, but the mistake is to unpin the Bishop again.

73 WHICH KNIGHT MOVES AND WHERE?

> Try 1 bS random (threat 2 cS any mate)
> 1 ... Rxd5 2 Sxd5 mate
> 1 ... Rc7! 2 ?
> Try 1 Sc4!? (threat 2 cS any mate)
> 1 ... Pb3 2 ?
> Try 1 cS random (threat 2 bS any mate)
> 1 ... Rxd5! 2 ?
> Key 1 Sb5! (threat 2 bS any mate)
> 1 ... Rxd5 2 Qa7 mate
> 1 ... Rc7+ 2 Sc4 mate
> 1 ... Pb3 2 Qa4 mate

Remove one Knight, and there is a Q+S battery – or remove the other Knight, and there is a different Q+S battery. Which is the right one? This *half-battery* idea took the problem world by storm in the 1960s.

74 WHICH ROOK MOVES AND WHERE?

Try 1 bR random (threat 2 cR any mate)
1 ... Be7+ 2 Rc5 mate
1 ... Bg5 2 Re3 mate
1 ... Be1 2 Qd8 mate
1 ... Bf6! 2 ?
Try 1 bRd4!? (threat 2 cR any mate)
1 ... Be1! 2 ?
Try 1 cR random (threat 2 bR any mate)
1 ... Be7! 2 ?
Key 1 Rc5! (threat 2 bR any mate)
1 ... Bf6 2 Rd4 mate
1 ... Bg5 2 Rf4 mate
2 ... Be1 2 Qd8 mate

Half-battery again (cf. *73*). Why not the overwhelmingly strong 1 Rxh3? Black is stalemated!

75 LUCKY SEVEN!

Key 1 Rd6! Waiting
1 ... Bf6 2 Qe4 (*A*), 2 Qe3 (*B*) and 2 Qe2 (*C*) mate
1 ... Bxb2 2 Qe4 (*A*) and 2 Qe3 (*B*) mate
1 ... Bf4 2 Qe4 (*A*) and 2 Qe2 (*C*) mate
1 ... Bxd6 2 Qe3 (*B*) and 2 Qe2 (*C*) mate
1 ... Bc3 2 Qe4 (*A*) mate
1 ... Bxg3 2 Qe3 (*B*) mate
1 ... Bd4 2 Qe2 (*C*) mate
1 ... Pd4 2 Rc3 mate

In *16* and *70*, a Black Knight and Pawn forced the *seven combinations* ABC, AB, AC, BC, A, B and C from three threatened mates labelled A, B and C. Here, the combinations flow from the seven moves of the Black Bishop.

D

76 COMBINATIVE SEPARATION

>   Key 1 Qxc7! Waiting
>   1 ... Rh6 2 Qe5 (*A*), 2 Qf4 (*B*) and 2 Sg5 (*C*)
>   mate
>   1 ... Rg6 2 Qe5 (*A*) and 2 Qf4 (*B*) mate
>   1 ... Rf6 2 Qe5 (*A*) and 2 Sg5 (*C*) mate
>   1 ... Re6 2 Qf4 (*B*) and 2 Sg5 (*C*) mate
>   1 ... Rxb6 2 Qe5 (*A*) mate
>   1 ... Rxd5 2 Qf4 (*B*) mate
>   1 ... Rc6 2 Sg5 (*C*) mate
>   1 ... Sc4 2 Qxc4 mate
>   1 ... Sb5/c2 2 Qxc2 mate

If 75 fascinated you, here is *combinative separation* by a Black Rook.

For the mathematically minded, A. R. Gooderson has shown the 15 combinations ABCD, ABC, ABD, BCD, CAD, AB, AC, AD, BC, BD, CD, A, B, C, and D from 15 moves of a Black Queen in reply to a four-fold threat. His problem, with 15 pieces (!) is just outside the scope of this book.

77 CHANGED SELF-PINS

>   Key 1 Pe3! (threat 2 Rf4 mate)
>   1 ... Qxf5 2 Qh1 mate (set 2 Qh4 mate)
>   1 ... Rxf5 2 Qa8 mate (set 2 Qe5 mate)
>   1 ... Sxe3 2 Sd2 mate

Ever popular with solvers is *Black self-pinning*. A problemist would not fail to investigate what happened after 1 ... Qxf5 and 1 ... Rxf5 in the diagrammed position, and the pin-mates he would want to see are 2 Qh4 and 2 Qe5. 1 Pe3! has the surprise effect of *changing* the mates after the two self-pinning moves which are now defences against the threat of 2 Rf4 double checkmate. The new pin-mates, again with the Black Queen and Rook held at f5, are 2 Qh1 and 2 Qa8. Mates on the diagonal are necessary to reclaim f3.

78 A CHESS PROBLEM TABOO

>   Key 1 Pd4+!
>   1 ... Qd3 2 Rxd1 mate
>   1 ... dRd3 2 Rxb1 mate
>   1 ... Sd3 2 Rxf3 mate
>   1 ... fRd3 2 Rxf4 mate

Checking keys are to be avoided by aspiring composers. A check is a natural continuation for a chess player, but problemdom demands a more subtle approach!

1 Pd4+! forces Black to make a quartet of *self-pinning* moves followed by four pin-mates (cf. 77). Especially interesting is that the key-move leaves the White Rook (f5) pinned by the Black Queen. 1 ... Sd3 and 1 ... fRd3 are unpins of this Rook which goes on to deliver mates dependent on the pin of the pieces which released it. Perhaps the tilt at convention is excused?

79 IS BLACK IN A TIGHT CORNER?

>   Key 1 Rh1! Waiting
>   1 ... Kh5 2 Kg3 mate (set 2 Pg4 mate)
>   1 ... Kf4 2 Re4 mate
>   1 ... B any 2 Qg5 mate

The answer to the caption is 'No – White is!' At least, that is the amusing visual effect of White's first move. The mate prepared for 1 ... Kh5 was 2 Pg4, but there is no waiting move for White to maintain this state of affairs. The hide-away key-move *changes* the mate to an attractive discovered mate by the newly formed R+K battery. Note that both the prepared mate 2 Pg4 and the post-key mate 2 Kg3 are pin-mates, with the Black Bishop immobilised.

80 ONCE A KNIGHT!

>   Key 1 Rh8! Waiting
>   1 ... Kf6 2 Pg8=S mate

It should be simple to mate Black who is so closely hemmed in by overwhelming White force, but the Black

King is too well guarded, and there is the danger of stalemate if White tries the obvious 1 Pg8=Q? There is no
mate in one move available to White, so the Black King
must go free temporarily before White mates on the stipulated second move. A try 1 Rg8? Kf6! 2 ? sees the Black
King go free, but there is no mating reply. The funny
key-move 1 Rh8! *relieves stalemate*, and avoids square g8
so that after 1 ... Kf6 2 Pg8=S is mate. It's all very simple,
but it is the sort of thing you remember.

81 RUNNING THE GAUNTLET

> Key 1 Qe4! Waiting
> 1 ... Kxe6 2 Re8 mate
> 1 ... Pd5 2 Pxd5 en passant mate
> 1 ... Pf5 2ePxf5 en passant mate
>   (2 gP xf5 e.p.?)
> 1 ... Pd6 2 Pxd6 mate
> 1 ... Pf6 2 Pxf6 mate
> 1 ... dPxe6 2 Qb7 mate (set 2 Qc7 mate)
> 1 ... fPxe6 2 Qh7 mate

'Running the Gauntlet' is the never bettered title of
a book devoted to *en passant* captures of a Pawn after its
two squares forward dash from its starting square. This
comparatively rare occurrence in over-the-board play has
been exploited to the full by problemists. This is a simple
but good example.

82 PAWN'S GAMBIT

> Key 1 Pd4! (threat 2 Kg3 mate)
> 1 ... cPxd4 en passant 2 Qxe4 mate
> 1 ... ePxd4 en passant 2 Qb7 mate
> 1 ... Bxd4 2 Qe1 mate

Unlike the Black Pawns' futile dashes in *81*, the White
Pawn's double jump key-move here is carefully calculated
to hasten Black's downfall by cutting the Black Bishop's
guard on h8 to threaten 2 Kg3 mate. To remove
the White Pawn, and re-open the Bishop's line to the
Rook, the Black Pawns capture *en passant*, but on arrival

at d3 the Pawns cut the c2 Bishop's guard on e4, and Queen mates at b7 and e4, according to the path opened by the capturing black Pawn, are possible. First 1 Pd4! and then 1 ... Bxd4 is a fine clearance sequence for 2 Qe1 mate!

83 AN OPEN AND SHUT CASE

Key 1 Bf4! (threat 2 Qf7 mate)
1 ... Kf5 2 Qg5 mate
1 ... Pc6 2 Qe6 mate
1 ... Pc5 2 Qg5 mate
1 ... Rf6 2 Qh7 mate
1 ... Rf5 2 Qg7 mate

The scheme is clear to the problemist. The Black Pawn at c7 will open the line of the Black Queen but will close the lines of the Black Rooks. It is also clear that White will threaten 2 Qf7 or 2 Qh7 mate (to guard the Black King's flight-square at f5) to force the Pawn's moves. 1 Bf4! stops short at that square to prevent 1 ... Qxe3, for example. The good try is 1 Bh4? (threat 2 Qh7 mate), but 1 ... Rh5! Two variations by the Rooks to block f5 and f6 are a bonus.

84 CHESS CHAMPION'S PROBLEM

Key 1 Qc3! (threat 2 Qb4 mate)
1 ... Ka3 2 Qa1 mate
1 ... Kb5 2 Qxc6 mate
1 ... Pe6 2 Qxb3 mate
1 ... Pe5 2 Qa5 mate
1 ... Rb5 2 Qa1 mate
1 ... Pc5/Rh4 2 Qa5 mate

David Pritchard is one of the strongest chess players in this country. Indeed, he is the author of 'Begin Chess' and 'The Right Way to Play Chess' in this Paperfront series. He has a number of excellent problems to his credit.

84 shows another aspect of the *Pawn Switch* of 83. The key-move, to give a second flight-square at a3, is first-class.

85 A QUEEN INTERPOSES

> Key 1 Qc7! (threat 2 Qc4 mate)
> 1 ... Kxh4 2 Qf4 mate
> 1 ... Bxe6+ 2 Qc4 mate
> 1 ... S any 2 Qg3 mate

Not easy to solve. 1 ... Bxe6+ 2 Bxe6 mate catches the solver's attention, and other moves by the Black Bishop are seen to be provided with mates 2 Pxf7 and 2 Pe7. Only 1 ... Pg5 leaves White without a mating reply. Surprisingly, the only way to mate Black is to play 1 Qc7! 1 ... Bxe6+ is not feared because the Black Bishop is pinned, and the threat 2 Qc4 mate still holds good by *interposal* on the check line. It takes courage to abandon the mates provided for Black Bishop moves in the initial position.

86 INTELLIGENT ANTICIPATION

> Key 1 Re3! Waiting
> 1 ... Kd8 2 Bb6 mate
> 1 ... Q any (Qg7+) 2 Rc3 mate
> 1 ... B any 2 Qxd7 mate

This bears comparison with 85. Only after moves of the line-pinned Black Queen has White no reply. The try 1 Re4? provides for 1 ... Q random on the rank (which opens the White Queen's guard to e8) by 2 Rc4 mate, but there is the easily overlooked checking refutation 1 ... Qg7+! The check at g7 is anticipated by 1 Re3! Now, all Black Queen moves, including 1 ... Qg7+, are answered by 2 Rc3 mate.

87 AN OLD-TIME SPECIAL

Key 1 Qf3 ! Waiting
1 ... Kb4/c4/d4 2 Se6 mate
1 ... Pb4 2 Qd5 mate
1 ... aS any 2 Qc3 mate
1 ... cS any 2 Sd3 mate
1 ... Pf6 2 Se6 mate

Who can fail to thrill to the opening move 1 Qf3 ! which takes the powerful Queen further away from the Black King, gives three flight-squares, and threatens nothing? The old-timers certainly knew how to make problems which appeal to ordinary chess players.

88 AT A STROKE!

Key 1 Qf6 ! (threat 2 Qxf5 mate)
1 ... Kd5 2 Qe6 mate
1 ... Kd3 2 Qd4 mate
1 ... Kf4 2 Rxg4 mate
1 ... Sd4 2 Qxd4 mate
1 ... B any 2 Bc2 mate

Like the previous problem, the White Queen gives the Black King three flight-squares e5, e3 and f4 at a stroke, but this time threatens to reclaim them immediately by 2 Qxf5 mate. Apart from the excellent key-move, the great merit of this problem is the provision of three *pin-mates* (cf. 77) after the Black King's moves.

Which of this and 87 is the more appealing? Joe Bunting's problem is a great technical achievement which can be better appreciated by the problem expert, but Alfred Challenger's has the move we would all have liked to have made.

89 DON'T CHEER TOO SOON

Key 1 Pe5 ! (threat 2 Qd3 mate)
1 ... Kxd5/d4 2 Qe4 mate
1 ... Bd4 2 Bb3 mate
1 ... Sd4 2 Se3 mate

But for the paradoxical reason that the key-move is too good, Andrew's problem might have pre-dated important Russian work which resulted in the principal variations being dubbed *Levmann*. How he missed out is seen from a comparison of this and *90*.

The generous key-move gives the Black King a second flight-square at d5, and threatens 2 Qd3 to reclaim both d4 and d5. Defences 1 ... Bd4 and 1 ... Sd4 are interposals on the Queen's prospective line of guard to d5 from d3, leaving the King free to escape at d5 if 2 Qd3?

90 LEVMANN DEFENCES

> Key 1 Sf3! (threat 2 Qd4 mate)
> 1 ... Kd5 2 Qe5 mate
> 1 ... 6Sd5 2 Sxd7 mate
> 1 ... 4Sd5 2 Sa6 mate
> 1 ... Bd5 2 Qxb4 mate
> 1 ... Pd5 2 Qf8 mate

The vital difference between this and *89* which might have robbed Britain of a 'first' is the additional effect of the four (!) Black defences to d5. They are *prospective unguards* of d6. The threat 2 Qd4 and the defences to d5 to close the Queen's line from d4 to d6 have a direct counterpart in *89*, but, additionally, the defences are made to tie the Queen to d6 which, unlike the corresponding square d5 in *89*, is not a flight-square unless White plays 2 Qd4?

91 POTENT PAWNS

> Key 1 Bg3! (threat 2 Pf3 mate)
> 1 ... Qxg3 2 Qb1 mate
> 1 ... Qf3 2 Pxf3 mate
> 1 ... Qe3 2 Pxe3 mate
> 1 ... Qd3 2 Pxd3 mate
> 1 ... Qb8 2 Pf4 mate

The White pieces have failed to stop the Black King (don't ask how it reached e1), so it is a blow for the little man that the Pawns are largely responsible for the mates. A Pawn threat 2 Pf3 brings the Black Queen to the defence, but she is picked off at f3, e3 and d3. After 1 ... Qb8 (a crafty move which stops both 2 Qb1 and 2 Pf3) the f-Pawn extends itself, 2 Pf4 mate!

92 *IDEAS ABOVE HIS STATION!*

Key 1 Ba5! (threat 2 Bc7 mate)
1 ... Ke5 2 Pd6 mate
1 ... Sc6 2 Pxc6 mate (set 2 Rxc6 mate)
1 ... Se6 2 Pxe6 mate

Pawn power was seen in *91*. Pawns are not to be under-rated. Even one Pawn so far up the board at d5 here is capable of mating Black three times!

1 Ba5! gives the Black King a flight-square at e5, but threatens 2 Bc7 mate. After Black King or Knight defences, the Pawn discovers checkmate from one or other of the Rooks. A good try is 1 Bd2? Sc6!

93 *SOLVERS OUT-GUNNED?*

Key 1 hRh2! Waiting
1 ... Qxf4 2 Rc2 mate (set 2 0–0 mate)
1 ... Qd2+ 2 Qxd2 mate
1 ... S any 2 Qxe3 mate

Did you spot the position of the White King and White Rook h1 and guess at *Castling*? It was the composer's intention that you should see 1 ... Qxf4 2 0–0 mate. And then were you stuck? That is what the composer wanted! The key-move 1 hRh2! clearly destroys Castling, but it lends support to the White Rook at e2 which gives a nice changed mate 2 Rc2 after being unpinned by 1 ... Qxf4.

94 *CASTLES IN THE AIR!*

Key 1 Rh4! Waiting
1 ... Pd3 2 Rxc4 mate (set 2 0–0 mate)
1 ... B moves 2 Sb3 or 2 Sd3 mate
1 ... Pe2 2 Bf4 mate

Knowing the solution to *93*, you will be getting wise to the tricks of chess problem composers, and Cyril Kipping's little piece of deception will not fool you for a minute – at least, I hope not! You will see 1 ... Pd3 2 0–0 mate, and that every Black move is provided with a mate. There is no simple waiting move, e.g. 1 Rg1? Pd3 2 0–0? to maintain the set mates. The startling 1 Rh4! provides a new mate 2 Rxc4 after 1 ... Pd3.

Can you make a problem with a Castling mate?

95 *WHY NOT P=Q CHECK?*

> Key 1 Qh7! (threat 2 Qxh8 mate)
> 1 ... Kb8 2 Qxh8 mate
> 1 ... Rg8 2 Qxg8 mate
> 1 ... Rf8+ 2 Pxf8=Q mate
> 1 ... Re8 2 Pxe8=Q mate
> 1 ... Rd8 2 Pxd8=Q mate
> 1 ... Rc8 2 Pxc8=Q mate
> 1 ... Rb8 2 Sc7 mate

This looks easy. 1 Pd8=Q+ Rxd8 2 Pxd8=Q mate and 1 Pe8=Q+ Rxe8 2 Pxe8=Q mate are two obvious solutions – so what's wrong? Another look, and you will see that 2 Pxd8=Q and 2 Pxe8=Q are illegal moves because the Black Rook *pins* the Pawn left on the seventh rank. It is a nice trap. Problemists call this arrangement a *White half-pin*: each White Pawn is 'half' pinned initially, and when one moves the other becomes fully pinned.

96 *TOO CLEVER BY HALF?*

> Key 1 Kb2! Waiting
> 1 ... Q any 2 Qxg4 mate
> 1 ... B any 2 Rxh3 mate
> 1 ... R any 2 Pxg3 mate

95 is the obvious way of showing the *White half-pin*. Alan's problem is much more subtle.

When it is seen that every Black move in the diagrammed position is answered by mate, a waiting move by White to solve the problem seems to be the answer. For example, try 1 Qe4? Waiting. Black replies 1 ... Be5! and the White Rook is pinned and cannot mate 2 Rxh3? Try 1 Rd3? Waiting – and the Black Queen plays 1 ... Qh8! Now, the White Queen is pinned and cannot play 2 Qxg4? The White Rook and Queen are *half-pinned*, but far from obviously!

97 *DRAW OFF THE CAVALRY*

Key 1 Sc8! (threat 2 Se7 mate)
1 ... Kd5 2 Sf4 mate
1 ... eSf5 2 Sxh4 mate
1 ... hSf5 2 Sxe3 mate
1 ... Sd5 2 Sa7 mate

The B+S *battery* at the bottom right-hand corner of the board is controlled by three Black pieces. If White tries an immediate 1 Sxe3+? or 1 Sxh4+? mate in two is prevented by 1 ... hSg2/f3! and 1 ... eSg2! respectively. The flight-giving key draws off the Black Knights by threatening 2 Se7 mate, and they cut the Black Bishop's line of guard onto the B+S battery. White takes the remaining Black Knight with mate. A nice touch is the blocking of the flight-square by 1 ... Sd5 when the key Knight has a second use, 2 Sa7 mate.

98 *EASTER EGGS YOU ON!*

Key 1 Se8! (threat 2 Qc7 mate)
1 ... Kd7 2 Qc7 mate
1 ... 7Sd5 2 Rxe3 mate
1 ... 3Sd5 2 Rxe7 mate
1 ... Pd5 2 Rc6 mate
1 ... Bxe6+ 2 Bxe6 mate

This time (cf. 97) a B+R *battery* is controlled by two Black Knights and a Bishop, but there is the added control of the White Rook (the firing piece of the battery) being pinned by the Black Bishop c4. The Knights' moves to d5 are *unpins* of the Rook which is then free to capture the remaining Knight controlling the battery. A third unpin of the Rook by 1 ... Pd5 is a good addition.

99 ALBINO

> Key 1 Kg7! Waiting
> 1 ... Rf4 2 Pf3 mate
> 1 ... Rxf5 2 Pf4 mate
> 1 ... Rg3+ 2 Pxg3 mate
> 1 ... Re3 2 Pxe3 mate
> 1 ... Rh3 2 Pf3 mate
> 1 ... Rxd3 2 Qb4 mate

The only Black piece free to move is the Rook, and it effectively suppresses the B+P battery. A carefully chosen waiting move 1 Kg7! (composers like to make good use of the White King) forces the Black Rook to move, and the striking effect is the four moves made by the White Pawn. To show there is no prejudice, the problemist's term for this is *Albino* – 62 was a *Pickanniny*.

100 ALBINO TWINS

> Try 1 Pe3? (threats 2 Qb7 and 2 dP any mate)
> 1 ... Rxe3 2 Pxe3 mate
> 1 ... Bc3 2 Pxc3 mate
> 1 ... Bd4 2 Pd3 mate
> 1 ... Rh4+ 2 Pd4 mate
> 1 ... Rf3! 2 ?
> Key 1 Pd3! (threats 2 Qb7 and 2 eP any mate)
> 1 ... Rxd3 2 Pxd3 mate
> 1 ... Bd4 2 Pe3 mate
> 1 ... Rf3 2 Pxf3 mate
> 1 ... Rh4+ 2 Pe4 mate
> 1 ... Bc3 2 Bxc3 mate

The last problem was a straight forward *Albino*. Much more complicated is this *half-battery* problem (cf. 73) with the four moves of a White Pawn doubled!

101 SHE STOOPS TO CONQUER

> Key 1 Qa3! Waiting
> 1 ... Sc7/b8 2 Sc7 mate
> 1 ... Sc5/b4 2 Qa8 mate

1 ... gS any 2 Sf6 mate
1 ... Pd6 2 Qa4 mate

The solver will want to keep the prepared mates 2 Sc7 and 2 Sf6 after Black Knight moves, but try as he will to find a key-move to preserve these mates unchanged, the only move which solves the problem is 1 Qa3! He need not fear 1 ... Sc5/b4 to close the Queen's line of guard on d7 (2 Sc7? is lost) because the surprising retreat to a3 is to play 2 Qa8 in the event. 1 ... Pd6 2 Qa4 is a pleasing *added mate*.

102 SMALL CHANGE

Key 1 Bd3! Waiting
1 ... aS any 2 Rb1 mate (set 2 Qxa2 mate)
1 ... cS any 2 Qh8 mate
1 ... Pc5 2 Qh1 mate

Like *101*, this is the type of problem by which Philip Williams is remembered. His problems usually had a few pieces attractively placed, mates after every Black move in the diagrammed position, and an element of the impossible. What White first move, for example, enables White to mate on his second in the manner indicated by the prepared mates? Good tries are 1 Rb3? aS any! 2 Qxa2? and 1 Ke5/f6? cS any! 2 Qh8? Only 1 Bd3! works. The *changed* but superior mate 2 Rb1 after 1 ... aS any is slight but charming.

103 INITIALLY 'JB'

Key 1 Be4! (threat 2 Qxe7 mate)
1 ... Kxe4 2 Re3 mate
1 ... Kd6 2 Qxe7 mate
1 ... Rxe4 2 Q/Rd5 mate
1 ... B/Sxe4 2 Bf4 mate
1 ... Bd6 2 Qf5 mate
1 ... Pe6 2 Qf4 mate

'JB' or John Brown of Bridport (1827–1863) was one of the earliest British composers to inject identity into their problems. His compositions broke new ground in that they were not the usual diffuse collections of mates of the period: they had definite ideas which could be labelled *themes*. 'JB's problem can be referred to as a *four-fold sacrifice* of a Bishop.

104 POLISHED OFF

> Key 1 Be4! (threat 2 Qd5 mate)
> 1 ... Kxe4 2 Re3 mate
> 1 ... Rxe4 2 Rxa5 mate
> 1 ... Bxe4 2 Pf4 mate
> 1 ... Rd4 2 Qe7 mate

Before the end of the 1800s, the new problem ideas with strong central ideas were being given polish and artistic finish by such notable composers as Godfrey Heathcote and Percy Blake whose constructional techniques are still an object lesson.

The basic similarity between this and *103* is readily identifiable. The reduction to 10 pieces, the pruning to essentials, and the sheer elegance of Heathcote's problem is an indication of his mastery.

105 PAST MASTER

> Key 1 Qb4! Waiting
> 1 ... Ke5 2 Qd6 mate
> 1 ... Bc3–a1 2 Sc3 mate
> 1 ... Bc5–a7 2 Sc5 mate
> 1 ... Bf6–h8 2 Sf6 mate
> 1 ... Bd5 2 Rf3 mate
> 1 ... Bxe3 2 Bg3 mate
> 1 ... Pe5 2 Qf8 mate

103 and *104* sketched the progress made from jumbles of mates to elegantly constructed and pointed positions. Slater's problem is a splendid example of the *development* of an art form. 1 Qb4! gives the Black King freedom at e5, and a trap is set for the Black Bishop which will be snapped up or shut off by the unmasked Q+S battery. Each time, the mating moves uncover the White Rook's line of guard to the flight-square e5. 1 ... Pf5 2 Qf8 is a brilliant finish.

106 UP FOR GRABS

> Key 1 Bxe6! Waiting
> 1 ... Kxe6 2 Rxe7 mate
> 1 ... Sc8 2 Bxc8 mate
> 1 ... Sd5 2 Bxd5 mate
> 1 ... Sf5 2 Bxf5 mate
> 1 ... Sg8 2 Bxg8 mate

In the diagrammed position, the only Black move is 1 ... S any, and this answered by 2 Rxe6 mate. Whatever White plays, this mate is lost. Don't try 1 Rxe7? because it is stalemate! The key-move 1 Bxe6! sacrifices the Bishop, but now the four Knight moves are answered by *grabs* by the Bishop. The problem's link with *105* is amusing. In *105*, a Knight grabs a Bishop; here, a Bishop grabs a Knight!

107 HINGES ON SQUARE B1

> Key 1 Qb7! Waiting
> 1 ... eS any 2 Rc2 mate (set 2 Qc2 mate)
> 1 ... Pc3 2 Sd3 mate (set 2 Sb3 mate)
> 1 ... dS any 2 Qb2 mate (set 2 Bb2 mate)

1Qb7! changes the mates after three Black moves, but what would otherwise be an ordinary achievement is elevated to a problem of distinction by the apparent choice of mates posed for White. Before the key, the correct mate is 2 Qc2 and not 2 Rc2? Kb1! after 1 ... eS any. It must be 2 Sb3 and not 2 Sd3? Kb1! after 1 ... Pc3. The different line of guard on b1 by the Queen when the key is made forces 2 Sd3 and not 2 Sb3? Kb1! after 1 ... Pc3, and 2 Qb2 not 2 Bb2? Kb1! after 1 ... dS any. Everything hinges on square b1.

108 THE RIGHT APPROACH!

>Key 1 Qg3! (threat 2 Qe5 mate)
>1 ... Rd6 2 Sc5 mate
>1 ... Bd6 2 Sd4 mate
>1 ... Rd5 2 Pxd5 mate
>1 ... Bf5+ 2 Pxf5 mate

It does not take long to see that the Queen will come into play to threaten 2 Qe5 mate. Black Rook and Bishop *Grimshaw* interferences (cf. *34*) at d6 to close the White Bishop's line result in mates 2 Sc5 and 2 Sd4. Wrong approaches are 1 Qa5? Rd6! 2 Sc5? Ke5! and 1 Qc3? Bd6! 2 Sd4? Ke5! Only 1 Qg3! is the correct *approach* when there is no danger of a Knight cutting a remaining line of guard on e5.

109 PRECISION PLAY

>Key 1 Qg2! Waiting
>1 ... Kxd3 2 Qe2 mate
>1 ... dRxd3 2 Rc5 mate
>1 ... dR else 2 Se5 or 2 Qxe4 mate
>1 ... bRxd3 2 Rb4 mate
>1 ... bR else 2 Sb2 or Qc2 mate
>1 ... Pe3/xd3 2 Qxd5 mate

Accurate play – always a single mate to finish off Black – is prized by problemists. Bristow's problem, with two Black Rooks free to roam the board, is a clever example. Mates after d–Rook moves are 2 Se5 or 2 Qxe4 (never both), and both are eliminated in favour of 2 Rc5 after 1 ... dRxd3. The b–Rook is used similarly to force accurate mates from the choice of 2 Sb2, 2 Qc2 and 2 Rb4.

110 THE ROOKERY

>Key 1 Qd8! Waiting
>1 ... Re8/e6 2 Qxd7 mate
>1 ... Rf7 2 Sxf7 mate
>1 ... Rg7/h7 2 Qf6 mate
>1 ... Rxe5+ 2 Bxe5 mate
>1 ... Ra6 2 Qxb8 mate

1 ... Rxb4 2 Bxb4 mate
1 ... bR else 2 Rc6 mate
1 ... B any 2 Qc7 mate

More play from two Black Rooks to compare with *109*. The excellent key-move unpins the e–Rook which forces an accurate choice from four mates 2 Qxd7, 2 Sxf7, 2 Qf6 (!) and 2 Bxe5. This, combined with the play from the b–Rook, makes a problem which deserves to be better known.

111 THE THIRD-DIMENSION

Set play 1 ... Bxe5 2 Qa8 mate   – *A*
          1 ... Pxe5 2 Qd8 mate   – *B*
Try Qg1? (threat 2 Qd4 mate)
1 ... Bxe5 2 Qxh1 mate   – *C*
1 ... Pxe5 2 Rd7 mate   – *D*
1 ... Sb4! 2 ?
Key 1 Qg4! (threat 2 Qd4 mate)
1 ... Kxe5 2 Qg5 mate
1 ... Bxe5 2 Qc4 mate   – *E*
1 ... Pxe5 2 Qd1 mate   – *F*
1 ... Be4 2 Qxe4 mate
1 ... Sb4 2 Ra5 mate

The improbable sounding *Zagorujko* is a frame-work for chess problem ideas, and derives from the work of a Russian, Leonid Zagorujko. Three different pairs of mates *AB*, *CD* and *EF* are shown in the set play, try play and post-key play after defences 1 ... Bxe5 and 1 ... Pxe5.

112 ZAGORUJKO

Set play 1 ... Kb5 2 Bd3 mate   – *A*
          1 ... Kd5 2 Be6 mate   – *B*
Try 1 Qg4? (threat 2 Qc4 mate)
1 ... Kb5 2 Qb4 mate   – *C*
1 ... Kd5 2 Qd4 mate   – *D*
1 ... Se4! 2 ?
Key 1 Qg6! (threat 2 Qc6 mate)
1 ... Kb5 2 Qb6 mate   – *E*
1 ... Kd5 2 Qd6 mate   – *F*

A *Zagorujko*, like *111*. This time, there are three different pairs of mates after the Black King's moves to b5 and d5.

113 OUT OF THE BLUE

Key 1 Pf3! Waiting
1 ... Pxb4 2 Qb5 mate
1 ... Pc4 2 Qe4 mate
1 ... cPxd4 2 Qa2 mate
1 ... ePxd4 2 Pc4 mate
1 ... Pe4 2 Pxe4 mate
1 ... Pxf4 2 Qe6 mate

One way of achieving *originality* in problem composition is to master the art of abstract thought. This involves casting out known ideas, and guessing at the unknown. Rather than sit, with head in hands, waiting for inspiration at an empty chess board, many composers like to be given a definite idea to work on. The basic instructions for *113* could have been 'show mates stemming from Black Pawn(s) moves'. Would you have matched the ingenious achievement of six different mates from the moves of two Black Pawns?

114 VARIATIONS ON A THEME

Key 1 Qh4! Waiting
1 ... Kc6/c5 2 Qc4 mate
1 ... Ke5 2 Qd4 mate
1 ... Pc6 2 Qd4 mate
1 ... Pc5 2 Qe4 mate
1 ... cPxd6 2 Sd4 mate
1 ... ePxd6 2 Bd7 mate
1 ... Pe6 2 Be4 mate
1 ... Pe5 2 Qc4 mate

What is said about *113* could apply here. Six mates flow from the moves of the two Pawns. Just like music, variations seem infinite.

115 THE LITTLE NUISANCE

> Key 1 Qe7! (threat 2 Qc5 mate)
> 1 ... Pd6 2 Qa7 mate
> 1 ... Pd5 2 Qa3 mate
> 1 ... Qxe7 2 Rf3 mate
> 1 ... Qe5 2 Qxe5 mate
> 1 ... Qe4 2 Qxe4 mate

Westbury's problem, which pre-dates an American classic, shows the Black Queen unpinned twice by the White Queen as it mates (cf. *67*). The Black Pawn is well meaning in its efforts 1 ... Pd6 and 1 ... Pd5 to stop the threatened 2 Qc5 (an unpin of the Black Queen, and nicely in keeping with the theme), but it is just a nuisance. The two unpins and mates 2 Qa7 and 2 Qa3 are due to the Pawn's interference.

116 NO FRILLS

> Key 1 Bb5! (threat 2 Ba6 mate)
> 1 ... Pd6 2 Qh8 mate
> 1 ... Pd5 2 Qh3 mate
> 1 ... Qc7+ 2 Pb7 mate

This may be seen as an effort to distil *115* to achieve a crystal-clear rendering without trimmings and with maximum economy. The essential variations 1 ... Pd6 2 Qh8 and 1 ... Pd5 2 Qh3 match those in Westbury's problem, and the snappy variation 1 ... Qc7+ 2 Pb7 mate springs beautifully from minimum force necessary to restrain the Black King.

117 NOW YOU SEE IT, NOW YOU DON'T

> Set play 1 ... R on file 2 Sxb6 mate – *A*
>   1 ... R on rank 2 Sc3 mate – *B*
> Key 1 Bc5! Waiting
> 1 ... R on file 2 Sf6 mate   – *C*
> 1 ... R on rank 2 Sc7 mate   – *D*
> 1 ... Rxc5 2 Sxb6 mate   – *A*
> 1 ... Pxc5 2 Sc3 mate   – *B*

Like the Zagorujko (cf. *111*), the *Ruklis* is a framework

for chess problems, and was inspired by another Russian, Dr. Efraim Rukhlis. The play is restricted to two phases (but it need not be), and the scheme of things is that the mates prepared for at least two Black moves in the diagrammed position disappear in favour of new mates – and then re-appear after different Black moves!

118 RUKHLIS

> Set play 1 ... 3S any 2 Se5 mate – *A*
>   1 ... 5S any 2 fSd6 mate – *B*
> Key 1 Bxd4! Waiting
> 1 ... Kxd4 2 Rb4 mate
> 1 ... 3S random 2 Sd2 mate   – *C*
> 1 ... 5S random 2 eSd6 mate   – *D*
> 1 ... 3Sxd4!? 2 Se5 mate   – *A*
> 1 ... 5Sxd4!? 2 fSd6 mate   – *B*

Another *Rukhlis* to compare with *117*. 1 Bxd4! spoils mates *A* and *B* prepared for both Black Knight moves, but by adding guards to c5 and c3 new mates *C* and *D* by the other White Knight become possible. Old friends, mates *A* and *B*, are seen again after flight-blocking captures of the Bishop.

119 A DEVILISH TRY

> Key 1 Bg2! (threat 2 Qe4 mate)
> 1 ... S random 2 Re6 mate
> 1 ... Sg7!? 2 Sd7 mate
> 1 ... Sd6!? 2 Rc5 mate
> 1 ... Sd4!? 2 Pf4 mate

1 Pf3 threatens 2 Qe4 mate. Lifting the Black Knight from the board (a *random move* letting through the Black Queen's guard) stops 2 Qe4, but the White Queen's line is opened as well, and 2 Re6 mate becomes possible. To stop both 2 Qe4 and 2 Re6 (the *secondary threat*), the Knight plays improved moves (*corrections*) to g7, d6 and d4. But what is the mate after 1 ... Qg7! which pins the White Queen? You have been caught. The real key is 1 Bg2!, a move which closes the potential pin-line.

120 BLACK CORRECTION

> Key 1 Qc3! (threat 2 Qxd4 mate)
> 1 ... Ke5 2 Qxd4 mate (set 2 Qe7 mate)
> 1 ... S random 2 Qxe1 mate
> 1 ... Sc2!? 2 Qd3 mate
> 1 ... Se2!? 2 Qe3 mate
> 1 ... Sxf3!? 2 Qxf3 mate
> 1 ... Sf5!? 2 Qe5 mate

The random and correction play of a Black Knight in *119* is seen again here. Both problems show *Black correction* mentioned already in connection with problems *53* and *54*. Eckett's problem shows three corrections, but David Shire goes one better with four!

121 ... WHERE ANGELS FEAR TO TREAD

> Key 1 Sc7! Waiting
> 1 ... Kxc7 2 Bh2 mate
> 1 ... Kxe7 2 Bc5 mate
> 1 ... Bxc7 2 Sc8 mate
> 1 ... Bxe7 2 Se8 mate

Composers are still discovering this quartet of mates. Guest's 1897 setting of the Black Bishop's blocks on the two flight-squares granted to the Black King by the key is still the best!

This leads to the question of how is a beginner to know what has been done before? Other than by a great deal of reading to get the 'feel' of what might or might not be new, and knowing sources of reference, it is largely guess work. By rushing in, beginners are frequently lucky!

122 A MEASURED TREAD

> Key 1 Rc6! (threat 2 Bb2 mate)
> 1 ... Se6 2 Bd6 mate
> 1 ... Sf5 2 Sg6 mate
> 1 ... Sd5 2 Sd7 mate
> 1 ... Se4 2 Pf4 mate

Apropos the last problem, the great T. R. Dawson (1889–1951) was the last person to 'rush in'. His was a *systematic approach* to problem composition based on a mathematical classification of the strategic elements and relative aspects of the pieces.

122 is an example of *horse-blocks* – a jargon name derided by Dawson – which shows the maximum of four blocking moves by two Knights on squares immediately next to the Black King.

No doubt, Dawson calculated that this combination needed to be shown, and he did it!

123 WHAT WE WANT

> Key 1 Rxg3! (threats 2 Sg6 and 2 Sf5 mate)
> 1 ... Sf6+ 2 Rg6 mate
> 1 ... Sg5+ 2 Rd3 mate
> 1 ... Sxg3+ 2 Sg6 mate
> 1 ... Sf2+ 2 Sf5 mate
> 1 ... Bg5 2 Rh3 mate

The cross-check sequence described in *11* and *12* remains ever popular because of the spectacular flourish afforded Black before White mates. It makes exciting chess. Exactly what we want is Watney's and Harley's *123*! 1 Rxg3! partially clears the Black Bishop's line to the White King, and the Black Knight makes four dangerous discovered checks. White's B+R and Q+S batteries are just sufficient to parry these checks with counter check and mate.

124 INTO THE THICK OF IT

> Key 1 Kb3! (threat 2 Qb4 mate)
> 1 ... Kd4 2 Sxc6 mate
> 1 ... Bc1–xg5+ 2 fSd3 mate
> 1 ... Bxf2+ 2 Sf3 mate
> 1 ... Bd4+ 2 eSd3 mate
> 1 ... Rb6+ 2 Qxb6 mate

It looks a suicidal move by the White King. The Bishop fires away with discovered check from the Black Rook at h3, but the White Knights fire back with deadly accuracy. Even the c–Rook has a shot, 1 ... Rb6+, but White's 'big gun', the Queen, picks it off, 1 ... Qxb6 mate.

Composed in blissful ignorance (cf. *121*) of what had been done in the cross-check field, the problem won top prize for the best problem by a British or Commonwealth citizen!

125 *ROTARY INTERNATIONAL*

Try 1 Sf1? (threats 2 Sh2/2 Sd2), 1 ... Qa2! 2 ?
Try 1 Sd1? (threat 2 Qg4), 1 ... Qc8! 2 ?
Try 1 Sc2? (threats 2 Se1/2 Sd4), 1 ... Qa1! 2 ?
Try 1 Sc4? (threats 2 Sd2/2 Se5), 1 ... Qa5! 2 ?
Try 1 Sd5? (threat 2 Re3), 1 ... Qe8/Sg3! 2 ?
Try 1 Sf5? (threats 2 Sd4/2 Sh4), 1 ... Qd8! 2 ?
Try 1 Sg4? (threats 2 Sh2/2 Se5), 1 ... Qb8! 2 ?
Key 1 Sg2! (threats 2 Se1 and 2 Sh4 mate)
1 ... Kg3 2 Se1 and 2 Sh4 mate
1 ... Pxg2 2 Qe3 mate

The *Knight wheels* away, but seven of its eight moves, and the bewildering variety of threats they pose, are countered by seven different moves of the Black Queen. A classic.

126 *A HORSE OF A DIFFERENT COLOUR!*

Try 1 Qc2? Waiting, 1 ... Sc3! 2 ?
Try 1 Qb1? Waiting, 1 ... 5Sb4! 2 ?
Try 1 Qa1? Waiting, 1 ... Sc7! 2 ?
Try 1 Qa4? (threat 2 Qxd7 mate), 1 ... Sb6! 2 ?
Try 1 Qe2? Waiting, 1 ... Se3! 2 ?
Try 1 Qf1? Waiting, 1 ... 5Sf4! 2 ?
Try 1 Qg1? Waiting, 1 ... Se7! 2 ?
Try 1 Qg4? (threat 2 Qxd7 mate), 1 ... Sf6! 2 ?
Key 1 Qb3! (threats 2 Q/Rxd5 mate)
1 ... 3Sb4/f4 2 Be5 mate
1 ... Sc7 2 Qb6 mate
1 ... 5Sb4 2 Rh6 mate
1 ... Se7 2 Qb8 mate

Compare *125*. The Black Knight plays to eight squares
to fend off eight moves by the Queen!

127 FLY AWAY PETER ...

Try 1 Bg5? Waiting, 1 ... Sxg8! 2 Pf5?
Try 1 Bf6? Waiting, 1 ... Sf5! 2 Qf6?
Try 1 Be7? Waiting, 1 ... Sxg4! 2 Se7?
Key 1Bd8! Waiting
1 ... Kh7 2 Bf5 mate
1 ... Sxg8 2 Pf5 mate
1 ... Sf5 2 Qf6 mate
1 ... Sxg4 2 Se7 mate
1 ... fS any 2 Rxh6 mate

Simply by moving the White Bishop h4, there is a
mate 2 Bf5 after 1 ... Kh7 when the Black Knight becomes
pinned by the Rook. But where precisely should the Bishop
move? 1 Bg5? ties the white Pawn to a guard of g5,
1Bf6? denies that square to the Queen, and 1 Be7?
stops a Knight mate. Only the fly away 1 Bd8! is correct.

128 ... COME BACK PAUL!

Try Pf4? (threat 2 Rg5 mate)
1 ... Sf3! and 1 ... Sh3! 2 ?
Try 1 Bf4? (threat 2 Rg5 mate)
1 ... Sf3! 2 ?
Try 1 hSf4? (threat 2 Rg5 mate)
1 ... Sh3! 2 ?
Key 1 gSf4! (threat 2 Rg5 mate)
1 ... Bxf4 2 Rxf4 mate
1 ... Sf3 2 Bh3 mate
1 ... Sh3 2 Pf3 mate

127 saw White fly to safety: this shows White roosting
at f4! Square f4 is an attractive perch because any move
there shuts the Black Bishop's line to g5, and 2 Rg5 is

mate. But which piece to f4? Only 1 gSf4! is correct. What a pity a *Rook* does not alight at f4!

129 COUNT DOWN

> Key 1 Qb6! (threat 2 Qc7 mate)
> 1 ... Ba4 2 Qf6, 2 Qd6 2 Qe6, 2 Sg6 and 2 Sd3 mate
> 1 ... Bb5 2 Qf6, 2 Qd6, 2 Qe6 and 2 Sg6 mate
> 1 ... Bxe4 2 Qf6, 2 Qd6 and 2 Qe6 mate
> 1 ... Bxd7 2 Qf6 and 2 Qd6 mate
> 1 ... Bd5 2 Qf6 mate
> 1 ... Rd5 2 Re7 mate

White makes progressively fewer mating moves after the five Black Bishop moves. There are an overwhelming five mates after 1 ... Ba4, four after 1 ... Bb5, right down to a single mate 2 Qf6 after 1 ... Bd5. It is a 5–4–3–2–1 progressive reduction! This modern theme is known as *progressive separation*, and may be compared with the combinative separation of *16, 75* and *76*.

130 HALF A DOZEN OF ONE ...

> Key 1 Bd5! Waiting
> 1 ... Kxg2 2 Sd2 mate
> 1 ... Ba7 2 Bxa7, 2 Bb6, 2 Bc5, 2 Bd4, 2 Be3 and 2 Bc4 mate
> 1 ... Bb6 2 Bxb6, 2 Bc5, 2 Bd4, 2 Be3 and 2 Bc4 mate
> 1 ... Bc5 2 Bxc5 2 Bd4, 2 Be3 and 2 Bc4 mate
> 1 ... Bd4 2 Bxd4, 2 Be3 and 2 Bc4 mate
> 1 ... Be3 2 Bxe3 and 2 Bc4 mate
> 1 ... Bxg1 2 Bc4 mate
> 1 ... Bxg3+ 2 Sxg3 mate
> 1 ... S any 2 Rxf2 mate

Like *129*, *progressive separation* of mates. 1 ... Ba7, the furthest of six moves by the Black Bishop on the long diagonal, prompts six mates by White, and, systematically, shorter moves reduce the number of mates to one.

131 AMBUSH!

> Key 1 Qf8! Waiting
> 1 ... Kf2 2 Sg2 mate
> 1 ... Rf2 2 Qa3 mate
> 1 ... Rxe2 2 Rxe2 mate
> 1 ... R else 2 Sg2 mate
> 1 ... Pxf4 2 Qxf4 mate
> 1 ... Pe4 2 Sd5 mate
> 1 ... S any 2 Qc5 mate

It hardly seems possible that a pull back of the White Queen to f8 will snare the Black King, but the retreat is a crafty ambush behind the White Knight. A good key!

132 THE OBLIQUE APPROACH

> Key 1 Qb5! (threat 2 Be7 mate)
> 1 ... Bd5 2 Qxb2 mate
> 1 ... Sd5 2 Qc6 mate
> 1 ... Ba3 2 Bd4 mate
> 1 ... Sg6 2 Sh7 mate

By hiding behind the Bishop and unpinning the Black Knight, the key is as devious as that of *131*. It would cause a stir if it occurred at the local chess club!

The threat 2 Be7 mate is interesting because the Bishop closes the Rook's line of guard to square e5, but opens the Queen's. 1 ... Bd5 is a subtle defence because it is a prospective closure of the Queen's line – if 2 Be7? Ke5! It is a small pity that 1 ... Sd5 is what problemists call *impure*, because the Black Knight guards e7 as well as closes the Queen's line.

133 WYNNE FOR WHITE!

> Key 1 Bc6! Waiting
> 1 ... Qg6 2 Rf2 mate
> 1 ... Qf6 2 Sd6 mate
> 1 ... Qxe6 2 Qf1 mate
> 1 ... Qf4–c1 2 6Sg7 mate
> 1 ... Q else 2 Rg5 mate
> 1 ... S random 2 Be4 mate

1 ... Sxe6!? 2 Qe4 mate
1 ... Pe4 2 Qd5 mate
1 ... Ph4 2 Qg4 mate

Containing the powerful Black Queen is a constant challenge for problemists (cf. *63* and *64*). Forced to move after the wonderful key 1 Bc6! the Queen clings doggedly to guards on g7 and g5, and only grudgingly lets in mates one at a time. Her moves to combat both 2 6Sg7 and 2 Rg5 are to g6, f6 and xe6, but the squares are blocked, and the Black King cannot escape after 2 Rf2, 2 Sd6 and 2 Qf1 mate.

134 *BANK ON SIR JEREMY!*

Key 1 Kg4! Waiting
1 ... Ke5 2 Sd7 mate
1 ... Qxg7+ 2 Bxg7 mate
1 ... Qxh8 2 Pxh8=Q mate
1 ... Qxf8 2 Pxf8=S mate
1 ... Qf7/h7 2 Pg8=S mate
1 ... Qe6/xd5 2 Pg8=Q mate

As in *133*, the Black Queen is the star performer. Her powers of movement along rank and diagonal are used to keep a potential flood of White Pawn *promotions* to a trickle. The promotions are twice to Queen and twice to Knight. Easily overlooked is that the fine key-move 1 Kg4! gives the Black King a flight-square at e5 and *pins* the White Pawn.

135 *BRIDGE THAT GAP!*

Key 1 Kf2! Waiting
1 ... Bxg3+ 2 Bxg3 mate
1 ... Bg5 2 Sxg5 mate
1 ... Bf6/xe7 2 Re3 mate
1 ... Pf4 2 Bf6 mate
1 ... cS any 2 Qd3 mate
1 ... bS any 2 Qd4 mate
1 ... Bb7/c6 2 Qxb7/xc6 mate
1 ... Bd5 2 Sd6 mate

The two-mover in the latter half of the 1800s developed from a nondescript collection of mates to a scheme with identity (cf *103*). Blake's elegant problem illustrates the process of transformation. It is not possible to say what is the central idea – is it the openings of the R+B battery, or the play from the Black Bishop h4? – but the theme beginnings are there.

136 *PENNY FOR HIS THOUGHTS!*

> Key 1 Re2! Waiting
> 1 ... Rc7+ 2 Kxc7 mate
> 1 ... Rc8 2 Kxc8 mate
> 1 ... Rc5 2 aSb6 mate
> 1 ... Rxc4 2 Qd7 mate
> 1 ... Rb6+ 2 Kxb6 mate
> 1 ... Ra6 2 Kxa6 mate
> 1 ... Rd6 2 Se3 mate
> 1 ... Re6 2 Qe4 mate
> 1 ... S any 2 Rd2 mate
> 1 ... Pf5 2 Rxe5 mate
> 1 ... Pe4 2 Qxe4 mate

With *135*, the struggle for identity in the two-mover was nearly won: Challenger's problem with its distinctive *theme* of eight variations from a Black Rook was an early winner!

137 *NEAR SYMMETRY*

> Try 1 Rf3? (threat 2 Rf5 mate)
> 1 ... Sc3+ 2 Rxc3 mate
> 1 ... Sf2+ 2 Rxf2 mate
> 1 ... Pd3 2 Rxd3 mate
> 1 ... Sd6! 2 ?
> Key 1 dRb3! (threat 2 3Rb5 mate)
> 1 ... Sb2+ 2 Rxb2 mate
> 1 ... Se3+ 2 Rxe3 mate
> 1 ... Sxb6 2 Rxb6 mate
> 1 ... Pd3 2 Rxd3 mate
> 1 ... Pxb3 2 Qa8 mate

A player would avoid unpinning Black, but a problemist jumps at the opportunity. Composers know this, and this problem is designed to give more than a moment's thought. If 1 dRb3! works, why should not 1 Rf3? in a near symmetrical setting? 1 ... eSd6! is not an obvious refutation of 1 Rf3? With minor adjustments, and the White Rook b6 moved to f6, 1 dRb3 would be the try (1 ... cSd6!) and 1 Rf3 the key!

138 OUT OF FOCUS

> Key 1 Kg6! Waiting
> 1 ... Rf6+ 2 Kxf6 mate
> 1 ... Rf7 2 Kxf7 mate
> 1 ... R else on file 2 Qb7 mate
> 1 ... Rg5+ 2 Kxg5 mate
> 1 ... Rh5 2 Kxh5 mate
> 1 ... R else on rank 2 Qh1 mate
> 1 ... Pc5/e5 2 Qb7 mate

Unpin of Black again, but unlike 55 it is not out of necessity to relieve stalemate. 1 Kg6! is finely judged move to put Black in Zugzwang. Black Rook moves other than to f7, f6+, g5+ and h5 are losses of *focal hold* (cf. 57), and either 2 Qb7 or 2 Qh1 mate results. A novel interpretation!

139 MASKED HALF-BATTERY

> Try 1 4Sa3? Waiting
> 1 ... Kxc5 2 Qc7 mate
> 1 ... cB moves 2 Sb4 or 2 Sd4 mate
> 1 ... S random 2 Qb6 mate
> 1 ... Sxc5! 2 ?
> Key 1 2Sa3! Waiting
> 1 ... Kxc5 2 Qd6 mate
> 1 ... cB moves 2 Sa5 or 2 Se5 mate
> 1 ... Bb7 2 Qd6 mate
> 1 ... aB else 2 Qc8 mate
> 1 ... S any 2 Qb6 mate

Did you recognise this as a *half-battery* (cf. *73* and
74)? The Black King is separated from the rear piece
of the half-battery, the White Rook, not by two pieces
but by four! The choice between 1 4Sa3? and 1 2Sa3!
is clear because of the need to guard b5 after the strong
Black move 1 ... Bb7.

140 GRAND CLEARANCE

    Position (*a*) Key 1 Rc5! Waiting
                1 ... dS moves 2 Rg1 or 2 Rb6 mate
                1 ... Sb2 2 aSc3 mate
                1 ... Sc1 2 eSc3 mate
                1 ... cS moves 2 Rg1 or 2 Rb6 mate
    Position (*b*) Key 1 Rc6! Waiting
                1 ... dS moves 2 Rf1 or 2 Rb5 mate
                1 ... Sb2 2 aSc3 mate
                1 ... Sc1 2 eSc3 mate
                1 ... cS moves 2 Rf1 or 2 Rb5 mate

As many pieces are piled on the *half-battery* line as
in *139*. First White, then Black, and then White again
clear the line to leave one or the other of the Black
Knights pinned – a grand clearance! A *dual* (two mates)
after 1 ... Se5 and 1 ... Sf4 in (a) disappears in (b).

141 OFF PAT!

        Key 1 Ke2! Waiting
        1 ... Ke6 2 Qe7 mate
        1 ... Kd4 2 Bf6 mate
        1 ... Kf4 2 Qd6 mate
        1 ... Pd4 2 Bc7 mate
        1 ... Pf4 2 Qf6 mate

This hitherto unpublished position was culled from
the scrapbook of the late William Marks of Northern
Ireland, one time chess editor of 'The Northern Whig'.
At the cost of a much less good key (1 Q(b4)–f8! in
Clark's problem gave two flights) four pieces are saved,

including a White Rook and Knight. The quartet of mates after Pawn and King moves to d4 and f4 is splendid.

142 GIVES THE GAME AWAY?

> Key 1 Qb4! (threat 2 Be1 mate)
> 1 ... Kd3 2 Qe4 mate
> 1 ... Kf3 Be1 mate
> 1 ... Kf2 2 Bd4 mate
> 1 ... Sf4 2 Bd4 mate
> 1 ... Sf2 2 Bd2 mate

There is a definite pointer to the key-move for the solver who remembers to look for Black moves which are so strong that White must give them immediate attention – see 'Hints for Solving'. 1 ... Sf4 shuts off the Queen from squares f3 and f2, and the Black King will go free. And what after 1 ... Kd3? 1 Qb4! is soon found. Even so, it is nice that the key-move to provide for potential flight-squares at f3 and f2 should grant them immediately!

143 MAKE WAY FOR HER MAJESTY!

> Key 1 Bh7! Waiting
> 1 ... Re7 2 Rd8 mate
> 1 ... R on file 2 Rf7 mate
> 1 ... Rxh7 2 Qxh7 mate
> 1 ... Sxb5 2 Qc8 mate
> 1 ... Sc6 2 Qxc6 mate
> 1 ... Pe5 2 Bf5 mate

Bishops have been excommunicated and even murdered, but there is spine-chilling *annihilation* for the Bishop at d3! Tries by the Bishop 1 Be2/f1? permit 2 Qxh7 after 1 ... Rh7 (the only Black move not provided with a mate initially), but 1 ... Pe5! becomes a defence. The startling 1 Bh7! clears the line for the Queen, a special type of clearance problemists call annihilation when the Bishop disappears after 1 ... Rxh7 to make 2 Qxh7 possible.

144   YOU WILL BE EXTERMINATED!

> Key 1 Qb8! (threat 2 Be5 mate)
> 1 ... Rh5 2 Sh3 mate
> 1 ... Rb4 2 Bf4 mate
> 1 ... Rb6 2 Bd6 mate
> 1 ... Rb7 2 Bc7 mate
> 1 ... Rxb8 2 Bxb8 mate

Annihilation to compare with *143*: the Queen clears to destruction for the Bishop.

A move by the Queen off g3 and out of the way of the Bishop threatens 2 Be5 mate from the R + B battery – but what move? Try 1 Qg4?, and the Black King escapes at h2 after 1 ... Rh5! 2 Sh3? Kxh2! Try 1 Qc7?, and the Bishop cannot reach round the Queen after 1 ... Rb8! Only 1Qb8! is correct in this original work – 1 ... Rxb8 and 2 Bxb8 mate!

145   MASTER MASTER ANDERSON!

> Key 1 Bd5! (threat 2 Qc4 mate)
> 1 ... Kxd5 2 Rg5 mate
> 1 ... Rxd5 2 Rxc1 mate
> 1 ... 6Sxd5 2 Sd7 mate
> 1 ... 4Sxd5 2 Se6 mate
> 1 ... Rd4 2 Qa5 mate

A sacrifice of a White piece always earns applause in over-the-board play, but problemists have become blasé about such moves. Gerry Anderson, another of Britain's Master composers, was a lad reading chess problem books under the desk when he made *145* – a *four-fold sacrifice*! The Black King and three other pieces capture the Bishop at their peril after 1 Bd5! threatens 2 Qc4 mate by adding a guard on c4.

146   WHITE GIVES UP!

> Key Rd6! (threat 2 Qd4 mate)
> 1 ... Kxd6 2 dSe4 mate
> 1 ... Bxd6 2 Qg1 mate

1 ... Sxd6 2 Qxa7 mate
1 ... Sc6 2 Rxc6 mate
1 ... Sxb5 2 cSe4 mate

Even before young Master Anderson was experimenting with sacrificial key-moves, B. G. Laws (1861–1931) was winning prizes by losing pieces! To the solvers of the day, 1 Rd6! – a *triple sacrifice* – was very daring, and what made the problem particularly attractive was the pair of Queen mates at either end of the a7–g1 diagonal.

Laws was one of the leading British problemists. and edited the problem section of the 'British Chess Magazine'.

Can you set out the pieces and Pawns to show a greater number of sacrifices?

147 NICE MATIN–G!

Key 1 Kd7! (threat 2 Se7 mate)
1 ... Qxa4 2 Sc7 mate
1 ... Qxe6+ 2 Qxe6 mate
1 ... Rxc6 2 Bxc6 mate
1 ... Se5+ 2 Qxe5 mate

The given theme was 'the key unpins one White piece and self-pins another. Black re-pins the first piece, but unpins the other which mates'. It sounds complicated, but Edward Beal's problem makes everything clear. 1 Kd7! unpins the White Knight c6 (no longer pinned by the Black Rook it can threaten 2 Se7 mate), but walks into a pin of the White Knight e6. 1 ... Qxa4 re-pins the White Knight c6 to stop the threat, but the White Knight e6 is unpinned, and mate 2 Sc7 becomes possible on the square vacated by the White King.

148 BITING THE HAND THAT FEEDS

Key 1 Qc5! (threat 2 Qf2 mate)
1 ... S random 2 Qxh5 mate
1 ... Sf4!? 2 Sg1 mate
1 ... Se3!? 2 Sd4 mate
1 ... Pd1=S 2 Se1 mate

E

The classic *Dalton* theme of this problem is to do with pinning and unpinning as is the more modern *Castellari* theme of *147*.

The formal requirements of a Dalton are that White piece A unpins Black piece B, and that the same piece B pins A. Here, the Queen unpins the Black Knight by its move 1 Qc5! to threaten 2 Qf2 mate. The released Knight finds that any move it makes stops the threat because the Queen is pinned by the Black Rook uncovered at h5 – there's gratitude!

149 RECORD BREAKER?

          Key 1 Bb3! Waiting
          1 ... Qxc2+ 2 Sxc2 mate
          1 ... Qxa2 2 Qxa2 mate
          1 ... Qxb3 2 Qxb3 mate
          1 ... Qc1 2 Qxc1 mate
          1 ... Qxe1 2 Qb2 mate
          1 ... Qa1 2 Qc5 mate

Unpinning of a White piece by a Black piece inter-fering on the pin-line was the theme of *17* and *18*. Here, the unpinning is by Black *withdrawal*. The Black Queen unpins by enforced withdrawal, and five different mates result. Only after 1 ... Qd1 is there an inaccuracy 2 Qb2 and 2 Qc5 mate, but this is excusable in this remarkable nine piece setting.

150 WITHDRAWAL METHOD!

          Key 1 Ra5! (threat 2 Qe3 mate)
          1 ... Bxd3+ 2 Qxd3 mate
          1 ... Bf3 2 Sc5 mate (not 2 Sf2? mate)
          1 ... Bg4 2 Sf2 mate (not 2 Sc5? mate)
          1 ... Bxa5 2 Rxf4 mate
          1 ... Be5 2 Rxe5 mate

This has only two *withdrawal unpins* to compare with the five of *149*, but they are more complex.

1 ... Bf3, the first withdrawal unpin of the Knight, closes the Queen's line to e3, and forces 2 Sc5 only –

2 Sf2? would close the remaining line of guard on e3 by
the White Bishop, and Black would escape 2 ... Ke3!
The second withdrawal unpin 1 ... Bg4 closes the Queen's
line to f5, and only 2 Sf2 is mate – 2 Sc5? would close
the Rook's line to f5.

151 *THROUGH THE LOOKING-GLASS*

  Position (*a*) Key 1 0–0! (threat 2 Sc7 mate)
       1 ... Pxa6 2 Rb8 mate
  Position (*b*) Key 1 Rxe3! (threat 2 Re8 mate)

 You saw in *6* and *21 Castling* as a legal or illegal move.
This twin problem has legal White Castling in position
(a) to stop legal Castling by Black out of danger (note
1 Rf1? Pd2 + !), but Castling by both Black and White
is made illegal in (b) by the tongue-in-cheek means of
mirror reflection of the diagrammed position i.e. the
White King and Rook stand at d1 and a1, and the Black
King and Rook at d8 and a8. There is no Castling away
from the threat in (b)!

152 *WHITE'S MOVE TO TURN!*

  Position (*a*) Try 1 Ke2? (threats 2 Sc3 and 2 Sa3 mate)
       1 ... Pe3! 2 ?
      Key 1 Sc3! (threat 2 Ke2 mate)
       1 ... Kh1 2 Ke2 and 2 0–0–0 mate
       1 ... Rxd2 2 Kxd2 mate
       1 ... Ra4 2 0–0–0 mate
       1 ... Pe3 2 Se2 mate
  Position (*b*) Try 1 Sf3? (threat 2 Kg5 mate)
       1 ... Re1 2 ?
      Key 1 Kg5! (threats 2 Sf3 and 2 Sf1 mate)
       1 ... Rxg4+ 2 Sxg4 mate
       1 ... Re3 2 Sf3 mate
       1 ... Re1 2 Sf1 mate

1 ... Ra4 2 0–0–0 mate is the surprise variation in posi-

tion (a) of this *half-battery*. Position (b) is created by a turn of the board which is another way of ruling out *Castling* (cf. *151*), but with the board rotated the Black Pawn's path is blocked, and 1 Kg5! is a key-move not possible in (a) because 1 ... Pe3!

153 RED INDIAN ...

> Key 1 Ra5! (threat 2 Qf4 mate)
> 1 ... Kxe4 2 Qf4 mate
> 1 ... Rxe4 2 Rxa3 mate

The visual effect of the key-Rook darting far to the left to ambush itself behind the Black Rook a4 in preparation for 1 ... Rxe4 2 Rxa3 mate caused a minor sensation when it was first shown by the American problem and puzzle king, Sam Loyd. The war-path of the key-piece led to it being dubbed the American Indian or *Red Indian* theme.

Sam Loyd's original problem was padded with many pieces to look like a game position (strictly against the rules for problemists!), and it took many solvers' scalps!

154 ... SLAUGHTERS WHITES!

> Key 1 Qb7! (threats 2 Qd7, 2 Qd5 and 2 Qf7 mate)
> 1 ... Ke6 2 Qd7 mate
> 1 ... Pxf3 2 Qd5 mate
> 1 ... Pxh5 2 Qf7 mate
> 1 ... Rg1 2 Qd7 mate

The link between this and *153* is tenuous, but *Red Indian* and *slaughter* really are problem terms.

Model mates have the squares immediately round the mated Black King guarded once only. Sometimes, to achieve these models of mates, Black obligingly captures or slaughters superfluous White pieces. This is seen twice in *154* when 1 ... Pxf3 and 1 ... Pxh5 make 2 Qd5 and 2 Qf7 mates by the skin of the teeth.

155 DOUBLE DOUBLE-CHECK BUT MATE!

> Key 1 Kc7! (threat 2 Kb8 mate)
> 1 ... Kg7 2 Kb8 mate (set 2 Ke6 mate)
> 1 ... Bxd6++ 2 Kxd6 mate
> 1 ... Bb6++ 2 Kxb6 mate
> 1 ... Sc8 2 Kxc8 mate
> 1 ... Sc6 2 Kxc6 mate

The fascination of Black being allowed to check White the move before White mates is strong, but when Black *double-checks* White twice, well . . .

The White King looks well placed because after 1 ... Kg7 there is 2 Ke6 mate, but it steps back to threaten 2 Kb8 mate. Massive broadsides from the Black Bishop checking at the same time as the pinned Black Rook are countered by captures at d6 and b6. It is a spectacular sequence.

156 WHITE DOUBLE DOUBLE-CHECKS

> Key 1 Kc6! (threat 2 Qd5 mate)
> 1 ... Qxe4+ 2 Qd5 mate
> 1 ... Qd3 2 Sd6 mate
> 1 ... Qc3 2 Sd2 mate
> 1 ... Qh5 2 Sxg3 mate

Less spectacular than the double-checks by Black in *155* are the *double-checks* by White in this problem, but they are no less ingenious. They come from White's R+S battery, so you can see that it is a typical problem move for the key 1 Kc6! to pin the Knight! 1 ... Qd3 and 1 ... Qc3 prevent the threatened 2 Qd5 mate, but the Queen's mistake is to unpin the Knight, and the battery opens for two double-checks – mates possible because the Black Queen blocks squares d3 and c3.

157 OF PRIME SECONDARY IMPORTANCE!

> Key 1 Qc8! (threat 2 Qe6 mate)
> 1 ... Kxc4 2 Qxc6 mate
> 1 ... cS random 2 Rh5 mate
> 1 ... Se7!? 2 Rxd6 mate
> 1 ... Se5!? 2 Sb6 mate
> 1 ... Sd4!? 2 Pe4 mate
> 1 ... Bxh6 2 Qg8 mate

The Knight corrects against the primary error of letting in 2 Rh5 mate, but makes *secondary errors* on arrival at e7, e5 and d4 (cf. *119* and *120*). Elegant!

158 ONE DEGREE OVER

> Key 1 Qc8! (threat 2 Qg8 mate)
> 1 ... Kxc4 2 Qxc6 mate (set 2 Qxd3 mate)
> 1 ... S random 2 Rxd3 mate
> 1 ... Sb4!? 2 Se3 mate
> 1 ... Sd4!!? 2 Sb6 mate

This problem takes *secondary Black correction* in *157* one step further to *tertiary Black correction*.

The primary error of 1 ... S random (to stop 2 Qg8 mate by making a potential flight-square at c6) is to unguard d4 – when 2 Rxd3 is mate. The correction 1 ... Sb4!? stops 2 Rxd3? but makes the secondary error of unpinning the White Knight by interference for 2 Se3 mate. A further correction 1 ... Sd4!!? corrects the primary error of letting in 2 Rxd3 and corrects the secondary error of unpinning the White Knight by stopping 2 Se3? because the Black Rook d3 is unpinned. The *tertiary error* is to block d4, and a new unpin mate 2 Sb6 becomes possible.

159 USING THE WHITE KING

> Key 1 Qd5! Waiting
> 1 ... gS random 2 Qf7 mate
> 1 ... Sxf3+!? 2 Qxf3 mate
> 1 ... Se6!? 2 Kxe6 mate
> 1 ... eS any 2 Sg3 mate

The Queen needs to control f7 and f3 for mates after 1 ... gS random and 1 ... Sxf3+. A try 1 Qb3! seems to *focus* these squares just as effectively as from b7, but 1 ... Se6! shuts off the Queen from f7. 1 Qd5! sets up a masked Q+K battery, and 1 ... Se6 is neatly answered by 2 Kxe6 mate. It is a small but charming problem to make good use of the White King.

160 EXPERTS BEWARE!

> Set play 1 ... B moves 2 Sf4 or 2 eSg7 mate
> Try 1 Bg5! Waiting
> 1 ... B moves 2 Sg3 or 2 fSg7 mate
> 1 ... Pxe6! 2 ?
> Key 1 Sg5! Waiting
> 1 ... B moves 2 Qe8 mate
> 1 ... P moves 2 Be8 mate
> 1 ... Qf3 2 Qxf3 mate
> 1 ... Qxe2 2 Bxe2 mate

You will see 1 ... B moves 2 Sf4 or 2 eSg7, and if you are an expert solver you will see immediately 1 Bg5 to change the *focal pair* to Sg3 and 2 fSg7 – but it's a trap. There is no mate after 1 ... Pxe6! 2 Qe8 is a real surprise after the key.

161 LINE CLOSURES

> Key 1 Sc4! Waiting
> 1 ... eS random 2 Se5 and 2 Pe5 mate
> 1 ... Sxg2!? 2 Se5 mate
> 1 ... Sxc4!? 2 Pe5 mate
> 1 ... Sd5+!? 2 Pxd5 mate
> 1 ... Sf5+!? 2 Pxf5 mate

Any White move to obstruct the Rook in the diagrammed position enables the Black King to go free at c5. How then can there be four mates which interfere with this Rook? When the Black Knight e3 moves, the Bishop g1 adds its guard to c5, and both 2 Se5 and 2 Pe5 mate. Checks at d5 and f5 result in Pawn captures of the Knight, and they are the third and fourth *interferences* on the Rook.

162 DETERMINED ON PROMOTION!

> Key 1 Sb5! Waiting
> 1 ... Pe1=Q 2 Pb4 mate (not 2 Sc3? mate)
> 1 ... Pe1=S 2 Sc3 mate (not 2 Pb4 mate)
> 1 ... Pxf2 2 Sxf2 mate

This is just one of a whole series of problem ideas based on White *closing White lines*.

After the key-move 1 Sb5 two potential mates are 2 Sc3 and 2 Pb4, but they are moves which cannot be played immediately as the line of the White Bishop to d2/e1 would be closed. Black must move, and the enforced Pawn promotions block e1 (as well as opening the Rook's line to d2), and Queen or Knight determine which interference White makes on the Bishop's line.

163 CHOICE OF PIN/UNPIN

> Try 1 2Rxd3? Waiting
> 1 ... Qc1/e1 2 3Rd4 mate
> 1 ... Qd1 2 Rc3 mate
> 1 ... Sxd5 2 Qxd5 mate
> 1 ... Qc2!
> Key 1 Sxd3! Waiting
> 1 ... Qc1 2 Se5 mate
> 1 ... Qe1 2 Sxb2 mate
> 1 ... Qc2 2 Rxc2 mate
> 1 ... S any 2 Qe4 mate

Withdrawal unpins of White by Black seen in *149* are extended to try-play. Will the Black Queen make withdrawal unpins of the White Rook (d2) or the White Knight after self-pinning captures at d3?

164 DO MEANS JUSTIFY END?

> Position (*a*) Key 1 Rd3+!
> 1 ... Kc4 2 Se5 mate
> 1 ... Ke4 2 Sf2 mate
> 1 ... Rd4 2 Rxd4 mate
> Position (*b*) Key 1 Rxb5+!
> 1 ... Kc4 2 Be2 mate
> 1 ... Ke4 2 Bf5 mate

163 shows a doubling of withdrawal unpin play in modern style: Colin Vaughan's problem has a bizarre doubling of *interference unpins* in ultra-modern style!

Position (a) starts with a controversial *checking key* 1 Rd3+! to force 1 ... Kc4 and 1 ... Ke4 which are moves to interfere with the Black Rook at a4, and to unpin twice the White Knight. A check in (b), too, forces the Black King to make interference unpins of the *Bishop* substituted at g4!

165 KEYED UP

> Key 1 Bc5! Waiting
> 1 ... Kd5 2 Sc3 mate
> 1 ... Kd3 2 Qb1 mate
> 1 ... B random 2 Qxc4 mate
> 1 ... Bd5!? 2 Qb1 mate
> 1 ... S any 2 Sc3 mate

There seems to be no sense in playing 1 Bc5! to shut out the Queen – especially when it is seen that the Black King has been given a second flight-square at d5. All that was called for was a simple waiting move to preserve the mates for all the Black moves in the diagrammed position. Try 1 Ba7? and 1 ... Sb6! (to give the Black King a flight-square at e3) foils White. The bombshell 1 Bc5! has delighted solvers since 1886.

166 CUT IT OUT!

> Key 1 Bd3! (threat 2 Bc3 mate)
> 1 ... Kxf6 2 Qh8 mate
> 1 ... Kd4 2 Qe4 mate
> 1 ... Rxd2 2 Qa1 mate

This problem shows that the old-timers had no monopoly of *good key-moves*, as might be suggested by *87* and *165*. Why the Bishop should drop to d3 and no further is baffling until the side-step threat 2 Bc3 is seen – the Black Rook is shut off from d4. The corner mates by the Queen are another pleasing feature.

This collection has served to save this little known gem from oblivion.

167 INVOLUNTARY REACTION

> Key 1 Qe8! Waiting
> 1 ... Sf8/c5 2 Qc6 mate
> 1 ... Sb6 2 Bxg4 mate
> 1 ... dSe5 2 Sc5 mate
> 1 ... gS random 2 Bxd7 mate
> 1 ... gSe5!? 2 Sf2 mate
> 1 ... B any 2 Qa8 mate
> 1 ... Pf5 2 Bd5 mate
> 1 ... Pxg5 2 Qg6 mate

By setting up a strong Q+B battery, and moving out of relative obscurity at d8, the Queen's move 1 Qe8! can be criticised, but in all other respects this is a perfect problem. The battery is controlled by two Black Knights, but unlike 97 and 98, their loss of control is involuntary. Forced to move by the Zugzwang situation, they give rise to beautiful play which includes the complementary pairs of mates 2 Bxg4/2 Bxd7 and 2 Sc5/2 Sf2.

168 SMEDLEY MEDLEY

> Key 1 Sxe4! (threat 2 Rc5 mate)
> 1 ... Bd6 2 Sd2 mate
> 1 ... Bd4 2 Sd6 mate
> 1 ... Pd6 2 Rc7 mate
> 1 ... Rd5 2 Rb6 mate

Unlike 167 and earlier examples, the B+S battery is controlled by two *line-moving pieces*, the Black Pawn d7 and the Black Rook. Instead of Black moves which abandon control of the battery, a carefully engineered threat 2 Rc5 mate causes the Black Bishop to cut either the Pawn's or Rook's line, and the Knight makes the other line-closure with mate.

169 WING FORWARD!

> Key 1 Ph4! (threat 2 Sf6 mate)
> 1 ... Kg4 2 Sf6 mate
> 1 ... Qxh4+ 2 Rh3 mate

    1 ... Qxf3+ 2 Bxf3 mate
    1 ... Qf5 2 Rxf5 mate
    1 ... Qe5 2 Re3 mate
    1 ... Qb1+ 2 Rf1 mate
    1 ... Qd4/f4 2 Rf4 mate

1 ... Qxh4+ 2 Rh3 mate is an *unpin/cross-check* variation which catches the attention to the extent that the four additional withdrawal unpins of the Rook by the Queen can be overlooked. It is far from obvious that these are *five withdrawal unpins* to compare with 149. 1 Ph4! to give the Black King a flight-square at g4 and to make a check possible at h4 is excellent.

170 PASSIVE RESISTANCE

    Key 1 Rf6! Waiting
    1 ... Bxe3+ 2 Bxe3 mate
    1 ... Bd4–a7 2 Qf8 mate
    1 ... Bd6 2 Re5 mate
    1 ... Bxe7 2 Rxe7 mate
    1 ... Bb4 2 Rc3 mate
    1 ... Ba3 2 Rxa3 mate

This little known problem bears resemblance to *169*, but it is more of a geometric exercise. Four of the Bishop's moves are *withdrawal unpins* of the White Rook resulting in a quartet of mates from the B+R battery: its remaining moves to keep the Rook pinned let in 2 Qf8 mate. Neatly, 1 Rf6! stops 1 ... Bd4 from being a defence against 2 Qf8 mate.

171 UPPER AND A DOWNER!

    Key 1 Qh8! Waiting
    1 ... Qe5/f6/g7 2 Qxe5/xf6/xg7 mate
    1 ... Qxh8 2 Pd4 mate
    1 ... Pc4 Pxc4 mate
    1 ... Pxb4 2 Rc7 mate

There seems no sense in the White Queen's climb to h8 to be hemmed in by the Bishop and Rook, but the reason is that the Black Queen must be drawn right away from the R+P battery. For example, 1 Qf6?, a move short of h8, results in 1 ... Qxf6! 2 Pd4? Qf3!, and no mate in two. After 1 ... Qxh8, the Black Queen may be unpinned with impunity, 2 Pe4 mate!

172 *ETERNAL TRIANGLE*

Key 1 Qa8! Waiting
1 ... aS any 2 Sc2 mate
1 ... Rxa3 2 Qh8 mate
1 ... Rb2 2 Bxb2 mate
1 ... Rc2 2 Sxc2 mate
1 ... dS random 2 Rxa2 mate
1 ... Sxb1? 2 Rxb1 mate

So cunning is the effect of 1 Qa8! that even after Black has played his a-Knight some would not see the mate 2 Sc2 – mate because the Rook is *pinned!* Another well hidden mate is after 1 ... Rxa3 when, with the Black Rook safely tucked behind the White Rook at b3, White can play 2 Qh8.

The Queen's corner to corner to corner triangular path is unforgettable!

173 *BLACK SEES STARS!*

Try 1 Sc3? Waiting
1 ... Kxf5 2 Bd3 mate
1 ... Kf3 2 Bd5 mate
1 ... Kh5 2 Be2 mate
1 ... Kh3 2 Bf1 mate
1 ... Pd5! 2 ?
Key 1 Bd5! Waiting
1 ... Kxf5 2 Sxd6 mate
1 ... Kf3 2 Sd2 mate
1 ... Kh5 2 Sxf6 mate
1 ... Kh3 2 Sf2 mate

Not one *star-flight*, as in 7, but two! Mates after the four Black King flights are changed.

174 PROCESS OF LOGIC?

> Try 1 S random (threat 2 gB any mate), 1 ... Ra2! 2 ?
> Try 1 Sf2!? (threat 2 gB any mate)
> 1 ... Kg8 2 Bd5 mate, 1 ... Kg6 2 Be4 mate
> 1 ... Ra6 2 Bc6 mate, 1 ... Rb5 2 Bd5 mate
> 1 ... Ra1 2 Bf1 mate, 1 ... Pe2 2 Bf3 mate
> 1 ... Pxf2! 2?
> Try 1 gB random (threat 2 S any mate), 1 ... Ra1! 2 ?
> Key 1 Bf1! (threat 2 S any mate)
> 1 ... Kg8 2 Sf6 mate, 1 ... Kg6 2 Sxe3 mate
> 1 ... Ra6 2 Sf6 mate, 1 ... Ra5 2 Se5 mate
> 1 ... Ra2 2 Sf2 mate, 1 ... Pe2 2 Se3 mate

Like *173*, this is a *half-battery*, but instead of roving off the line the Black King moves on it. The logical sequence by which the solver is led to 1 Sf2? as a try and 1 Bf1! as the key is called *White correction* (cf. *197*).

175 NICE ONE, CYRIL!

> Key 1 Qf3! Waiting
> 1 ... Qa5+ 2 Rb4 mate (set 2 Qxa5 mate)
> 1 ... Qa1+ 2 Rb1 mate (set 2 Qxa1 mate)
> 1 ... Qa6 2 Rxe8 mate
> 1 ... Qb6 2 Rxb6 mate
> 1 ... Qa4 2 Rb5 mate
> 1 ... Qb8 2 Ra7 mate
> 1 ... Qxb7 2 Qxb7 mate
> 1 ... S any Sc7 mate

32 is a duel between the Black Queen and the B+S battery: this shows a *Black Queen v. Q+R battery*. Moves by the Black Queen to stop 2 Rxe8 mate (the immediate effect of her losing control of the eighth rank) weaken her hold on the Q+R battery, and she becomes prey for the Rook either by capture or shut off. The changed mates after 1 ... Qa5+ and 1 ... Qa1+ make up for an aggressive key.

For many years, Cyril Kipping carried the banner of British problem chess.

176 DUEL TO THE DEATH

>   Key 1 Qe7! (threat 2 Qh4 mate)
>   1 ... S random 2 Be2 mate
>   1 ... Sxd1!? 2 Bxd1 mate
>   1 ... Sxd5!? 2 Bxd5 mate
>   1 ... Sxg4+!? 2 Sxg4 mate
>   1 ... Sxg2!? 2 Bxg2 mate

After *175*, the next contest is a Black Knight v. R + B battery. The best of four correction moves by the Knight (the random error is to let through the Queen to e2 for 2 Be2 mate) is 1 ... Sxd1!? The Black King will escape if 2 Be2? by 2 ... Ke1!

177 HALF-PIN DEMONSTRATION

>   Key 1 Bg5! (threat 2 Sf6 mate)
>   1 ... Kh5 2 Sf6 mate
>   1 ... Sh5 2 Qxe6 mate
>   1 ... Bf5 2 Qe2 mate
>   1 ... Sxg5 2 Qxg5 mate

The idea of this problem has proved to be one of the most fruitful in the history of problem chess. It shows the *half-pin* theme in its basic form of two Black pieces (here, the Bishop and Knight f4) between the Black King and a White line-moving piece (the White Rook a4). For the half-pin to be complete, each Black piece must move off the line, and there must be a mate dependent on the piece remaining on the half-pin line being fully pinned. After 1 ... Sh5, the Bishop e4 is left pinned, and 2 Qxe6 is mate: after 1 ... Bf5 the Knight is pinned, and 2 Qe2 is mate.

178 GREAT RE-DISCOVERY

>   Key 1 Sc5! (threat 2 Qf2 mate)
>   1 ... Ke1 2 Qf2 mate
>   1 ... Be3 2 Qd1 mate
>   1 ... Be1 2 Bd1 mate
>   1 ... Sd3 2 Qe4 mate
>   1 ... Sd1 2 Qxd2 mate

As in *177*, square-blocking by the Black pieces as they move in turn off the *half-pin* line a2–e2 plays its part in the mates with the remaining Black piece on the half-pin being fully pinned – 1 ... Be3 2 Qd1 and 1 ... Be1 2 Bd1. A third half-pin variation is 1 ... Sd3 2 Qe4 mate.

Grandmaster Mansfield brought the half-pin to prominence when still a young man, and coined the term in 1915.

179 UNIQUE COMBINATION?

> Key 1 Qd5! (threats 2 Qd2 and 2 Qg5 mate)
> 1 ... Bxd5 2 0–0 mate
> 1 ... Sxd5 2 Kf2 mate
> 1 ... Se4 2 Qd1 mate

Here is the *half-pin* of *177* and *178* with *Castling*. The combination seems to be new – which is astonishing after the attention given to the theme this century.

The thematic variations are 1 ... Bxd5 2 0–0 mate (Castling is forced to avoid the reach of the Bishop, and the Black Knight c3 is pinned), and 1 ... Sxd5 2 Kf2 mate (Castling through check is illegal, and the Bishop c4 is pinned).

180 OUT OF THE RUNNING?

> Key 1 eSc5! (threats 2 Be6–a2 mate)
> 1 ... Rxa4+ 2 Ba2 mate (set 2 Qxa4 mate)
> 1 ... 0–0–0 2 Sb6 mate
> 1 ... Be6 2 Bxe6 mate
> 1 ... Bh7 2 Qd7 mate

What is the Knight doing so far away at a4? Even if it is unpinned by the Black Rook, it cannot reach the Black King. But if the Black Rook *unpins* the Knight at the same time as the Black King moves – *Castles*! – the Knight leaps in with mate 2 Sb6! The Black King is released for Castling by the key 1 eSc5! which also changes the prepared mate after 1 ... Rxa4+ from 2 Qxa4 to 2 Ba2, a cross-check.

181 THE FRENCH CONNECTION

Key 1 Se7! Waiting
1 ... Ke5 2 Qe1 mate
1 ... B random 2 Rd5 mate
1 ... Be5+!? 2 Rd6 mate
1 ... Bd4!? 2 Re3 mate

157, for example, might give the impression that *Black correction* can only be played out by a Black Knight. In this little known problem from a French theme tourney the Black Bishop shows its paces.

The primary error of 1 ... B random is to open a second White guard on f3, and 2 Rd5 is mate. One correction is 1 ... Be5+!?, but the secondary error is to block the flight-square, and 2 Rd6 is a cross-check mate. The second correction 1 ... Bd4!? stops 2 Rd5, but a new secondary error blocks d4 – when 2 Re3 is mate.

182 TAKEN TO TASK

Key 1 Be8! Waiting
1 ... Kc4 2 Qc3 mate
1 ... R random on file (d8) 2 Kb3 mate
1 ... Rd6!? 2 Qc3 mate
1 ... Rd4!? 2 Qc6 mate
1 ... Rd3!? 2 Kxd3 mate
1 ... Rd2+!? 2 Kxd2 mate
1 ... Rd1!? 2 Kxd1 mate

Not to be outdone by the Black Bishop of *181*, the Black Rook makes what might be a *record five corrections* to d6, d4, d3, d2+ and d1 to stop 2 Kb3 mate.

This record or near record type of problem is the speciality of Sir Jeremy Morse who is one of the world's leading authorities on *tasks* – problems with maximum effects.

183 UNDERHAND TRICKS

Position (*a*) Key 1 Pe8=S! (threat 2 Sxf6 mate)
1 ... Kg8/h8 2 Sxf6 mate
Position (*b*) Key 1 Pe8=B! (threat 2 Bg6 mate)
1 ... Kg8/h8 2 2 Bg6 mate

Here's a funny one in which White relieves *stalemate* by *under-promotion* to Knight in position (a) and to Bishop in (b). The really notable feature, however, is the *twinning device* of the removal of the Black Pawn at f7 to create position (b). Twins are common now, but 100 years ago they were rare.

Although better done since (a present day composer would switch the Queen for a Rook, and remove the White Pawn c7, etc.) this goes to show that there is not much new under the sun!

184 STILL GOING STRONG

> Key 1 Qe8! (threats 2 Pf8=Q, 2 Pf8=S,
>   2Pxg8=Q and 2 Pxg8=S mate)
> 1 ... Se7 2 Pf8=Q mate
> 1 ... Sxf6 2 Pf8=S mate
> 1 ... Pxf6 2 Pxg8=Q mate
> 1 ... Ph5 2 Pxg8=S mate

More than 100 years on from *183*, White *Pawn promotion* is still the theme. Mansfield's problem shows relatively modern *threat separation* (cf. *65*). The key 1 Qe8! sets up a Q+P battery which threatens four promotions by the Pawn, twice to Queen and twice to Knight, but the four moves Black has force White to make a careful choice from these promotion possibilities.

185 MUCH ADO ABOUT NOTHING!

> Key 1 Qe7! Waiting
> 1 ... Kg6 2 Qxf7 mate
> 1 ... Kxf4 2 Qf6 mate
> 1 ... Pf6 2 Qe4 mate
> 1 ... Bxf4 2 Be4 mate
> 1 ... 6B else 2 Qg5 mate
> 1 ... Bg6 2 Qe5 mate
> 1 ... 5B else 2 Qxf7 mate

'JB's role in the development of the two-move problem is referred to in *103*. This gem shows the firm foundations on which he built.

The problem's slender means of 9 pieces – from which 7 mates are extracted – highlights a *curious difference* between the problemist and player. A player starts with 32 pieces, but the problem composer begins with an empty board. It's his job to make much ado about nothing!

186 ANCIENT BRITONS

> Key 1 Qh2! Waiting
> 1 ... Rh8+ (Rg3) 2 Qxh8 mate
> 1 ... Rf3/R else 2 Sxf3 mate
> 1 ... Pg4 2 Qf4 mate
> 1 ... S any 2 Sc2 mate

This is another old favourite. The key-move 1 Qh2! to preserve the mates of the diagrammed position must have been a real teaser. Normally, such waiting moves to keep Black in Zugzwang are colourless.

Frank Healey (1828–1906) was another of the *early British composers* to make pointed problems ahead of their time ... see 'JB's *185* and Healey's *45*.

187 NO WANDERING MINSTREL HE!

> Key 1 Ba2! (threat 2 Se2 mate)
> 1 ... Kg5 2 Qe5 mate
> 1 ... Rxc3 2 Sg6 mate
> 1 ... Rxc1 2 Se6 mate
> 1 ... Rd2 2 Qc5 mate
> 1 ... Bg5 2 Be6 mate
> 1 ... Bf6+ 2 Qxf6 mate

The Soviet chess problem historian and International Master composer, E. I. Umnov, has described Grandmaster Mansfield as the *minstrel of battery play*, the recurring theme of Mansfield's work for more than 65 years. The core of this early masterpiece is the pair of battery mates 2 Sg6 and 2 Se6 after the Black Rook has destroyed guards on e5 and g5 by captures 1 ... Rxc3 and 1 ... Rxc1. Well in keeping with the idea is the battery opening threat.

188 OLD SCHOOL TIE

> Key 1 Sg4! Waiting
> 1 ... Ke6 2 Sd4 mate (set 2 Qf7 mate)
> 1 ... Kc4 2 cSe5 mate
> 1 ... bS random 2 Qb3 mate
> 1 ... Sc4!? 2 Sd8 mate
> 1 ... gS random 2 Qf7 mate
> 1 ... Se6!? 2 cSe5 mate

A composer whose name and work is little known is W. T. Hurley. His problem is taken from the magazine of St. Joseph Williamson's Mathematical School, Rochester, *'The Williamsonian'*, in which Hurley edited a chess column.

The problem is built round the Q+S battery openings.

189 MUTATION

> Key 1 Ba6! Waiting
> 1 ... Kc6 2 Qxe6 mate
> 1 ... R random on file 2 Bb7 mate (set 2 cSb6 mate)
> 1 ... Re7!? 2 Sxe7 mate
> 1 ... R else 2 Se7 mate
> 1 ... S any 2 Qc4 mate

A *mutate* in problem chess is a Zugzwang position changed to another with at least one changed mate. The mates prepared for 1 ... R any are 2 cSb6 and 2 Se7, but with White to play there is no way of keeping both mating replies. 1 Ba6! creates another Zugzwang position, and the replies to Rook moves are now 2 Bb6 and 2 Se7. There is only one changed mate, but it is most attractively done. 1 ... Kc6 2 Qxe6 is an added mate.

190 IT MAKES A CHANGE!

> Key 1 Sb8! Waiting
> 1 ... Kc5 2 Qc6 mate
> 1 ... Rc5 2.Qe6 mate (set 2 Sxb4 mate)
> 1 ... Pf4 2 Qh5 mate (set 2 Qe4 mate)
> 1 ... R else 2 Qb5 mate

Another *mutate* to compare with *189*, but with two changed mates. If it were Black's turn to play, among the mates prepared for all Black moves would be 2 Sxb4 and 2 Qe4 after 1 ... Rc5 and 1 ... Pf4. Only 1 Sb8! solves the problem by creating a new Zugzwang position. The mates after 1 ... Rc5 and 1 ... Pf4 are changed to 2 Qe6 and 2 Qh5.

Mansfield's classic *57* is a mutate.

191 THE SIDEBOARD KEY!

> Set play 1 ... S random 2 Qf3 mate
>   1 ... Sg4!? 2 Qf7 mate
> Try 1 Qc4? Waiting
> 1 ... S random 2 Qe2 mate
> 1 ... Sg4!? 2 Qf7 mate
> 1 ... Sd3! 2 ?
> Key 1 Qa4! Waiting
> 1 ... S random 2 Qd1 mate
> 1 ... Sg4!? 2 Qe8 mate

Move the Black Knight unthinkingly, and the Queen mates 2 Qf3. Play the Knight to g4 to block the diagonal, and the Queen mates 2 Qf7 – and so on with changed mates after try and key-move. Almost a Zagorujko (cf. *111*)!

192 FOUR-WAY-PLAY

> Key 1 Qb5! (threat 2 Qb3 mate)
> 1 ... S random 2 Bd4 mate
> 1 ... Sb6!? 2 Qxa5 mate
> 1 ... Sd6!? 2 Qe5 mate
> 1 ... Sxb2!? 2 Qxb2 mate

After 1 ... Sb6 and 1 ... Sd6 to stop 2 Qb3 and the secondary threat of 2 Bd4 after 1 ... S random, the line opening and closing effects are: 1 ... Sb6 (i) opens Black line g8–b3, (ii) closes Black line c7–a5, (iii) opens White line b5–d3, and (iv) closes White line a7–d4 – and mate 2 Qxa5 results. 1 ... Sd6 (i) opens Black line g8–b3, (ii) closes Black line c7–e5, (iii) opens White line b5–d3, and (iv) closes White line d7–d3 – and mate 2 Qe5 results. This is *four-way-play* doubled.

193 TELL TALE ROOK

> Key 1 Qe8! (threat 2 Rf4 mate)
> 1 ... Kg6 2 Rf6 mate (set 2 Se5 mate)
> 1 ... Kxg4 2 Qe2 mate
> 1 ... Bxg4+ 2 Rf3 mate
> 1 ... Rxg4 2 fRxh7 mate
> 1 ... Bf6/h6 2 Rg7 mate

Although the White Rook f7 is part of the mating net in the set variation 1 ... Kg6 2 Se5 mate, its isolation at f7 is the clue to the key 1 Qe8! which sets up a Q+R battery. The threat 2 Rf4 reclaims the flight-square g4 given by the Queen's move. The *switchback* mate 2 Qe2 – the Queen returns to her starting square – is good.

194 GIVE A LITTLE, TAKE A LITTLE

> Key 1 Sd2! (threat 2 Rd5 mate)
> 1 ... Kxd2/d3 2 Rd5 mate
> 1 ... Pe1=Q+ 2 Rf1 mate
> 1 ... Pe1=S 2 Rc5 mate
> 1 ... Pxd2 2 Rf3 mate
> 1 ... Bxd2 2 Rb5 mate

1 Sd2! gives a flight at d2 and takes a flight at b3 – a *give-and-take* key – and unpins the Pawn at e2 which becomes a Queen with check to the White King. 2 Rf1 mate is an excellent cross-checking reply, and one of five openings of the B+R battery.

195 WAS HE FIRST?

> Key 1 Qb6! (threat 2 Qf2 mate)
> 1 ... Ke1 2 Qb1 mate
> 1 ... S random+ 2 Rb2 mate
> 1 ... Se2+!? 2 Rg7 mate
> 1 ... Ph1=S 2 Qg1 mate

The Queen's move off the masked line of the Black Bishop bearing on the White King enables the Black Knight to move with check. To stop 2 Rb2 after 1 ... S random (the Rook must hold square e2) the Knight blocks the line to b2, but it also blocks e2, and 2 Rg7 is a complement-ary cross-check.

Was Sparke the first to show this classic *cross-check* pair? A 1st prize in the Good Companion Club of problem world experts the world over seems to favour his chances.

196 ASSOCIATION OF IDEAS

> Key 1 Qd7! Waiting
> 1 ... Sxd7+ 2 Rg8 mate
> 1 ... Se6+ 2 Pf8=S mate
> 1 ... Sxg6+ 2 Pf8=Q mate
> 1 ... Rg8 2 Pxg8=Q mate
> 1 ... Pg3 2 Qh3 mate

Many of the problems in this book are combinations of ideas, and this blending of favourite themes of *cross-checks* and *promotions* is a good example. A Queen move off the top rank seems to tempt fate by exposing the White King to discovered checks, but 1 Qd7! is quite safe (not 2 Qe7? Pg3!). There are three *cross-check promotion* mates from the Q+P and B+R batteries. Black did the Queening in *194*, but White does it here!

197 DISTURBING THE PIECE!

> Try 1 Sa3? Waiting
> 1 ... dS any 2 Sc2 mate (set 2 Rxb5 mate)
> 1 ... fS any 2 ?
> Try 1 Sb6? Waiting
> 1 ... fS any 2 Sd5 mate, 1 ... dS any! 2 ?
> Try 1 Se3? Waiting
> 1 ... dS any 2 Sc2 mate
> 1 ... fS any 2 Sd5 mate, 1 ... Sxb3! 2 ?
> Try 1 Sb2? Waiting
> 1 ... Sxb3 2 Rxb3 mate
> 1 ... fS any 2 Sd3 mate, 1 ... dS any! 2 ?
> Key 1 Se5! Waiting
> 1 ... dS any 2 Sc6 mate
> 1 ... Sxb3!? 2 Rxb3 mate
> 1 ... fS any 2 Sd3 mate

This is *White correction*, and a counterpart to *Black correction* in *53*, for example. It is the process of logic a player experiences when he seeks the right square from many for a White piece to be moved.

198 SAFETY PINS

> Key 1 Sd6! (threat 2 Qb4 mate)
> 1 ... Ka3 2 Qxb3 mate
> 1 ... Qa3 2 Qb5 mate (set 2 Sxc3 mate)
> 1 ... Qxc2 2 Sc5 mate

In the many Meredith problems examined for this book, there is nothing to compare with Colin Sydenham's three *line-pin mates* 2 Qb4, 2 Qxb3 and 2 Qb5. 1 Sd6! shuts out the Black Bishop to threaten mate by the Queen still pinned. 1 ... Ka3 unpins the Black Rook to make 2 Qb4? impossible as a mate, but the Black Queen is pinned, and the White Queen slides a little further down the pin-line for 2 Qxb3 mate. 1 ... Qa3 blocks the flight-square to make possible a third line-pin mate 2 Qb5 with the Queen still immune from capture!

199 DEDICATED TO LONDON TRANSPORT

> Key 1 Kg3! Waiting
> 1 ... S random 2 Qc7 mate
> 1 ... Sb6!? 2 Qb4 mate
> 1 ... B any 2 Qxb5 mate
> Try 1 Kxg4? Bc8+! 2 ?

It is no accident that the pieces form the shapes of the letters *LT*. The problem was made for London Transport's chess magazine.

Successful *letter problems* are difficult to make as predetermined places for the pieces put enormous constraints on the composer. Most examples have rather weak play, but they are composed and published in the party spirit. Recently, the Dutch Master composer, Jac Haring, sent four problems to spell out the letters *BCPS* to mark the Jubilee of the British Chess Problem Society's magazine!

200 *LATE DEVELOPMENT PAYS!*

> Key 1 Ra5! (threats 2 Rb5 and 2 Bd2 mate)
> 1 ... Kxa5 2 Bd2 mate
> 1 ... Sxa5 2 Ba3 mate
> 1 ... Sc4 2 Qa4 mate

Finally, a bit of fun – and a challenge!

Chess players can hardly fail to notice that the bottom rank is occupied by six White pieces on their *original squares*. To say the least, White's development is retarded! Even so, 1 Ra5! is mate in two. It is an inspired bit of nonsense, but there is the underlying seriousness that each White man is absolutely essential, and that there is a unique key-move.

Can you make a problem to equal or better this?

Composer Index By Problem Numbers

Index to Problem Ideas and Strategies

'The Problemist' is the quarterly magazine of the **British Chess Problem Society,** and is devoted to all aspects of problem chess. The British Chess Problem Society exists to promote the knowledge and enjoyment of chess problems, and membership is open to problemists in all countries. The annual subscription is:

Ordinary Members	£2.50
Fellows	£5.00

and runs from January 1st each year. Payment should be made to the Hon. Secretary and Treasurer, G. W. Chandler, 46 Worcester Road, Sutton, Surrey SM2 6QB, England; the Society's National Giro Account No. is 337 0151, and banker's order forms may be obtained if required.

SOME OF OUR OTHER BOOKS

OUR PUBLISHING POLICY

HOW WE CHOOSE

Our policy is to consider every deserving manuscript and we can give special editorial help where an author is an authority on his subject but an inexperienced writer. We are rigorously selective in the choice of books we publish. We set the highest standards of editorial quality and accuracy. This means that a *Paperfront* is easy to understand and delightful to read. Where illustrations are necessary to convey points of detail, these are drawn up by a subject specialist artist from our panel.

HOW WE KEEP PRICES LOW

We aim for the big seller. This enables us to order enormous print runs and achieve the lowest price for you. Unfortunately, this means that you will not find in the *Paperfront* list any titles on obscure subjects of minority interest only. These could not be printed in large enough quantities to be sold for the low price at which we offer this series.

We sell almost all our *Paperfronts* at the same unit price. This saves a lot of fiddling about in our clerical departments and helps us to give you world-beating value. Under this system, the longer titles are offered at a price which we believe to be unmatched by any publisher in the world.

OUR DISTRIBUTION SYSTEM

Because of the competitive price, and the rapid turnover, *Paperfronts* are possibly the most profitable line a bookseller can handle. They are stocked by the best bookshops all over the world. It may be that your bookseller has out of stock of a particular title. If so, he can order more from us at any time—we have a fine reputation for "same day" despatch, and we supply any order, however small (even a single copy), to any bookseller who has an account with us. We prefer you to buy from your bookseller, as this reminds him of the strong underlying public demand for *Paperfronts*. Members of the public who live in remote places, or who are housebound, or whose local bookseller is unco-operative, can order direct from us by post.

FREE

If you would like an up-to-date list of all paperfront titles currently available, send a stamped self-addressed envelope to
ELLIOT RIGHT WAY BOOKS, BRIGHTON RD.,
LOWER KINGSWOOD, SURREY, U.K.